For Elizabeth and to all of the men and women who protect us from those who would do us harm.

PERSONAL SECURITY

Preparing for the Unexpected in an
Era of Crime and Terrorism

Richard Bradford

CONTENTS

PREFACE

All of us should prepare for the unexpected.

This book was originally conceived as a supplement to counterterrorism courses for personnel traveling to hostile areas. Therefore, some of its content is meant primarily for those who might be specifically targeted for terrorist or other criminal violence. These individuals are often chosen for attack because of their occupation and/or nationality. For those likely to be singled out for assault, subjects such as route analysis, surveillance detection, and high performance driving have been included. Those who believe they may fall into this category should study the entire book.

Increasingly others are targeted, not because they have a particular job or because of their nationality, wealth, religion, race, or gender, but because they are "soft" (relatively unprotected and vulnerable) targets of opportunity. It often serves the terrorists' purpose to attack such targets indiscriminately to magnify fear and panic.

Most recent victims of terrorist or other criminal violence have simply been in the wrong place at the wrong time. They were either targets of opportunity or collateral damage in an incident primarily aimed at others. Many of the techniques included here also apply to avoiding or evading these terrorist attacks, everyday crime, and simple accidents. These threats make anyone and everyone a potential victim.

The focus here is on *personal* security. Although the book was not specifically intended for individuals who are assigned a protective detail nor for members of such a detail, both could benefit from it.

Paradoxically, the individual specifically targeted for attack has some advantages over the more randomly selected target of opportunity. Tactics, including route analysis and surveillance detection, designed to uncover pre-attack indicators can serve to warn the specifically targeted person. The person who simply goes to a restaurant, theater, concert, mall, sporting event, or other public place does not have the opportunity to discover the pre-attack surveillance that may have been conducted there for days, weeks, or months before the attack.

Those most concerned with preparing for possible target of opportunity attacks, should focus on the following chapters:

INTRODUCTION
PRINCIPLES AND PHILOSOPHY
HABITS
THE ATTACK CYCLE
THE COLOR CODES
OBSERVATION SKILLS
AWARENESS AND ANALYSIS

DRIVING HABITS
COMMENTARY DRIVING
EPILOGUE

All of us should prepare for the unexpected.

INTRODUCTION

This book does not follow the traditional approach to personal security. That approach suggests preparing for a large range of possibilities rather than the more reasonable approach of concentrating on demonstrated probabilities.

Personal security is often taught by those with backgrounds in law enforcement or the armed forces. Superficially this makes a great deal of sense. Firearms and close quarters combat are often seen as the primary skills necessary for personal protection. Typically, military personnel and police officers receive the most training and have the most experience in firearms and close quarters combat. Naturally, they tend to teach the skills with which they are most expert. The expectation is that their students will somehow apply these skills as the solution to an undefined problem. Statistically, however, these responses are usually inappropriate and are very rarely used (or useful) in avoiding, evading, or even in countering an actual attack. We believe it is more useful to determine what the threat is likely to be and what skills are necessary to elude that threat. We have attempted to do that with our courses and with this book.

TRADITIONAL APPROACH

LOCATION

Where are attacks most likely to occur? Often personal security courses, articles, and books concentrate on incidents at the victim's residence and at the workplace. This seems logical if you consider that most of a typical day is spent at these two locations.

Residential security is important. Most of us practice residential security without giving it a second thought. There was a time in this country when most people did not lock their doors. Times have changed. We almost all do now. Dogs, alarms, gated communities, and neighborhood watch programs are extensively used now. Statistically, such an attack is less likely than other types, because of these safeguards. There is a wealth of literature available on how to better secure your home. You can read that for yourself. We urge you to do so.

Attacks against individuals at the work place are most often carried out by someone known by the victims and usually result from a perceived grievance. That is not the type of attack we will address here.

Outside forces could also attack your workplace. History includes many examples of this type of attack, often against government facilities. This is the type of attack in which the facility itself, the organization the facility represents, and the groups inside are the targets. Examples include the Oklahoma City Federal Building, various US State Department facilities, private corporations, churches, and non-government organizations (NGOs). Along with coworkers, you can use the information and techniques in THE ATTACK CYCLE and SURVEILLANCE DETECTION chapters to help foil an attack on your workplace. Here you have teamwork advantages unavailable in other venues.

History tells us that well over 80 percent of attacks against specifically targeted individuals take place when that individual is in transit – in or near a vehicle. It is not when you are in your home or workplace that you are most vulnerable. You are more conspicuous and vulnerable in a vehicle than in a building.

CATEGORIZING THE THREATS

A common approach to personal security training is to categorize possible threats and treat each category as a separate subject. Using this technique, you would study terrorism, sexual assault, carjacking, kidnapping, burglary, murder, robbery, domestic violence, etc. separately. This approach is often used by those instructors with analytical or police backgrounds. They are accustomed to classifying threats. One problem with this approach is that it may slow your response to an attack. Unconsciously you will still be categorizing and analyzing the threat instead of reacting to it. At the time of the attack, knowing that your attacker intends to injure or kill you is all the analysis of motivation needed.

TRADITIONAL RESPONSES

Two types of response are favored by traditional personal security instructors - martial arts and firearms.

MARTIAL ARTS

Martial arts may be helpful in countering an attack. Statistically, however, it is unlikely. Martial arts certainly provide additional capabilities but they are capabilities that should be addressed only after all of the more basic, statistically more relevant, skills have been mastered. If your only objective is self defense, then your time could be better spent mastering techniques that are more likely to prove useful prior to rather than during an attack.

FIREARMS

I began teaching personal security as a firearms instructor. After several years of firearms training and, more importantly, after studying what actually happens in "the field," I determined that, like martial arts, it is a nice-to-have additional skill. Almost everyone (other than military personnel or police officers) would be better off first learning other, more basic, avoidance skills that are more likely to save their lives.

ADDRESSING PROBABILITIES – NOT POSSIBILITIES

One problem with the traditional martial arts and firearms approaches is that they tend to address possibilities rather than probabilities. It is possible that we might be able to protect ourselves by using martial arts or firearms but it is not probable that they will be the most relevant or effective techniques. Presumably the attack plan will not allow the target the proximity to use hand-to-hand maneuvers or the time to draw and use a firearm. In any case, if we must resort to the use of hand-to-hand self-defense or firearms we have failed to avoid and failed to evade the threat that we are now forced to counter.

Perhaps the most important disadvantage of the martial arts and firearms approaches is that they are only effective in countering an attack. They provide no help in avoiding or evading a threat. Successfully avoiding or evading renders any countering technique unnecessary.

REACTIONS TO ATTACK

Some of our students have expressed concern that they might over react to a perceived threat. Actually, under reaction is a more probable response. This may be in part because of our inability to believe that we are being attacked. One of the most common comments of victims interviewed after an attack is, "I couldn't believe it was happening."

Many victims of sudden violent attack do nothing. Their greatest and possibly only error is that they have never imagined being attacked. Unfortunately, many of them die. One study of reactions in a number of catastrophic incidents makes it possible to predict what people will do when endangered. The study shows that 10 to 15 percent will react calmly and reasonably. It is notable that many of these will have either trained for such an incident or experienced a somewhat similar incident in their past. Approximately 15 percent will panic (over react). The remaining 70 to 75 percent will do little or nothing (under react). (Ripley, 2005.)

THE IMPORTANCE OF EFFECTIVE HABITS

Statistically the likelihood of an unsuspecting victim surviving a planned attack is less than one in ten. In contrast, the likelihood of a targeted person, who is not immediately killed, surviving a planned attack in cases where that victim does something, is greater than nine in ten. This includes cases where the survivor did something which, in hindsight, would seem to have been the wrong thing. We can conclude that, in most cases, even doing the "wrong" thing is better than doing nothing at all.

I have watched many students revert to ineffective habits in cases where they clearly knew intellectually that their response was incorrect (or would have known if they had actually thought about it). For example, in one course, we provided several days of high performance driving training. Included in the training was the importance of keeping both hands on the steering wheel. We then pitted groups of students against each other in a pursuit exercise. The student driving the lead car would drive around a figure-eight track as rapidly as possible, attempting to increase the gap between the two cars. The driver of the pursuing car would attempt to close the gap. Most students drove right at the limit of adhesion (as fast as they could drive the car without inducing a skid), some drove beyond that limit, producing dramatic skids and losing control of their vehicle. For the students the adrenaline rush was real. In spite of their previous training, I have seen students who had "mastered" the mechanics of high performance driving, steering with one hand on the wheel and the other on their lap. The students had not practiced the new way of driving long enough or often enough for it to override their old driving habits.

As another example, we introduced an exercise into one of our courses in which students would be surprised by a carjacking attempt. This exercise was conducted after repeated reminders to the students to lock their car doors and keep the windows up. Despite repeated admonitions, in many cases the driver's door was unlocked and the assailant was able to open the door and directly threaten the driver. One of the teaching points was that the driver should have locked his door, giving him time to escape as the assailant was trying to get it open. In several cases not only did the assailant open the unlocked door, he was able to force the driver out of the car, get in himself, and drive off. Many of these students habitually relied on the fact that their own cars locked automatically. They were not in their own cars for this exercise.

TACTICS VS. PRINCIPLES

It would be nice to be able to provide a list of tactics and techniques that could be applied to a wide variety of possible threats. Many have already offered this "solution." To do so may be a disservice. A tactic applicable in one environment may be disastrous in another. In the carjacking example above, when we critiqued the students' response we pointed out the error in leaving the door unlocked. We also noted that if the assailant did open the door and was in the driver's face with a gun, it clearly made sense for the driver to give up the car. Certainly the car was not worth dying for. We then started including in our debriefing of the students that giving up the car was the right response – assuming that the car was unlocked. Within a few weeks of our decision on how to deal with this situation, terrorists in the Middle East began kidnapping and beheading people they captured. The car is still not worth dying for. Doing everything possible to avoid decapitation is worth the effort.

There is no substitute for each person learning what the risks are in the particular environment in which he will find himself. There are many sources of this information. As illustrated in the example above, the response to a carjacking may be very different from the response to attempted murder. You must know which you are likely to face and that depends on the local threat environment.

If we cannot offer universally applicable techniques, we can offer some principles. (Often the problem is distinguishing between techniques and principles.) The remainder of this book will deal with those principles.

As I have told countless students in hundreds of classes – simply knowing the proper way of handling a situation is meaningless in the chaos of an attack. Regardless of what you consider to be the logical response to a surprise violent assault, what you do, if you do anything at all, will depend on habit. It will be unthinking and automatic. In fact, it is preferable that your response be unthinking and automatic. The question is, will your response be to freeze? Will your actions be based on inappropriate habit?   Or, will you respond appropriately and survive?   No proper response will be automatic and habitual if it has not been practiced.   You must practice the skills we will address in order to make them habitual.

> You must practice until the desired response is automatic.

PRINCIPLES AND PHILOSOPHY

"One is not exposed to danger who even when in safety is always on their guard."

Pubilius Syrus

Prepare for the most likely threat.

The first principle we will apply is to devote the greatest part of our preparation to the most probable threat.

PRINCIPLES VERSUS CASE STUDIES

As instructors, many of our discussions center on the analysis of actual incidents. The ultimate goal is to uncover the universal principles with which to form the basis for the students' mindset, and intuition, and, hopefully, to provide a model for their reactions to various potential threats. We must make training scenarios as realistic as possible but, at the same time, with the greatest range of applicability. No matter how many case studies we analyze or scenarios we develop, none will exactly duplicate the conditions that a student will later encounter in the "real world." Our approach here is to concentrate on presenting principles that can be applied to the greatest number of probable incidents. In this book we purposely avoid presenting case studies or many historical examples. While the principles presented here are drawn from actual incidents, we have not described those incidents in detail. Doing so could detract from the primary lessons that the incidents impart and burden the reader with irrelevant, unimportant, or misleading information.

MINDSET

Perhaps the most important goal of personal security training is to develop the proper mindset. This means that we must realize that it is possible that we will be targeted for attack and decide that we are going to do something about it. For many people this may be an alien concept. An attack launched against the average (unsuspecting) victim is very likely to be successful (from the attacker's point of view) for several reasons.

FACTORS THAT FAVOR A SUCCESSFUL ATTACK

Being unsuspecting, the target is unlikely to be aware of the potential dangers. Not knowing the threat, the target is unlikely to be looking for the indicators that could warn of the imminent attack. Even if an indicator is noticed, it is unlikely to be recognized for what it is.

> Expect to be attacked.

Having failed to notice the warning signals, the victim is going to be surprised when the assault takes place.

12

Even if the victim has a few seconds to react, time will be wasted on his first attempt to understand what is happening, convince himself that it is actually happening, develop a response, and then attempt to execute that response.

Too often the assault is completed before the victims are able to do anything other than stare in disbelief. They have searched their minds to find a solution and found nothing useful. Those without training are the most likely to freeze – unable to comprehend what is happening or what to do about it. This "training" may, at a minimum, consist of imagining threats and visualizing their response.

> Imagine threats. Visualize responses.

PHYSIOLOGICAL RESPONSE

If you are suddenly and violently attacked, you will encounter another obstacle – the physiological response. Along with a significant increase in heart rate, the body will respond with a flood of chemicals. You will almost certainly experience any or all of the following as your heart rate increases:

At about 115 beats per minute (BPM):
Motor skills: Fine motor skills begin to deteriorate.
At about 155 BPM:
Motor skills: Complex motor skills begin to deteriorate.
At about 175 BPM:
Hearing: Auditory exclusion.
Seeing: Loss of near vision, tunnel vision, Loss of depth perception
Thinking: Cognitive processing deteriorates.
Above 175 BPM:
Motor skills: Gross motor skills at highest level of performance.
Other: Freezing, Submissive behavior, Vasoconstriction, Voiding of bladder and/or bowels

In addition you may experience:

Dry mouth
Difficulty in talking and/or swallowing.
Cool, clammy, sweaty skin.
Tightening of the scalp (hair seems to stand up).
Rapid breathing.
Heightened arousal and vigilance.
Inhibition of the processing of pain.
Distorted perception of time.
Dilated pupils.

The physiological factors (chemical and automatic) are such that you may be unable to carry out a response, even if you are able to formulate one.

> Develop responses that take the physiological factors into account.

If we could develop a response that took advantage of the unavoidable physiological responses and possibly even the psychological ones it would certainly be preferable. It is difficult to imagine anything that would require a greater degree of fine and complex motor skills than the aiming and firing of a weapon, particularly a handgun. We know that the vision required for aiming and the motor skills required for trigger control will be significantly diminished in the stress of a violent assault. When the physiological factors are taken into account it is not surprising that there are so many misses in a gunfight.

Critics could charge that our approach is too simple. I would counter that, to be workable, it must be simple. Even if the target of an attack is physiologically capable of executing a complex response, most people are unable to devote the time needed to master such a response.

> Keep it simple.

The basic philosophy of personal security can be stated in three words.

```
AVOID
EVADE
COUNTER
```

AVOID

It may seem facetious, but the easiest solution is to avoid the threat. If you suspect or know that there will be an incident at a given time and place, do not be there.

A great deal of the literature on personal security has been based on military or police experience. Generally, military forces are expected to kill or capture their enemies and to seize terrain. Police are required to make arrests. Therefore, their tactics are designed to accomplish those offensive tasks. The rest of us usually have the luxury of avoiding trouble - assuming we are aware of it.

Often cultural influences cause us to fail to listen to our own suspicions. We may have a vague feeling that things are not right but we often ignore it. We may go to a dangerous part of town because we refuse to allow thugs to dictate how we live our lives. We may chase a thief because we refuse to be taken advantage of.

Much of the knowledge you may need is local. It is impossible to provide that knowledge in a course designed to provide general guidance that is applicable world-wide. Obtaining this information is a personal responsibility. For example, if carjacking is a common crime in a given part of the world, giving up a car when threatened may be a perfectly reasonable response to a carjacking attempt. No car is worth dying for. However, if hostage taking and the execution of hostages is a very real problem in your area, then the appropriate response will be very different.

Study all of the information available about threats in the area. Include as many sources as possible, to include internet searches, books, articles, and questioning others who are in or have recently been in the area of concern.

Know and avoid the most likely threats in your area.

EVADE

If you have failed to avoid the threat, your next best option is to evade it. You suffer from several disadvantages if you failed to avoid. Now you must somehow escape from a threat that you did not recognize in time to avoid.

Evading requires skills. (Avoiding would only have required knowledge – not skill.) In a vehicle you are restricted to two choices – move forward or move backward. The thing to remember is the single word "move."

Our reaction to an attack must be planned. In fact, in order to be timely, it must be habitual and automatic. Hearing or reading about an appropriate response is not sufficient. You must practice that response (or at least practice it by repeated visualization) until it becomes an automatic and habitual reaction. No matter how good you think a certain technique may be, you will not use it if you have not rehearsed by at least thinking about it frequently.

| Practice |

COUNTER

If you have failed to avoid or evade a threat, your final option is to counter it. If evading requires some skill, countering requires even more. All of the requirements for practicing, visualizing, and rehearsing discussed above under EVADE apply to countering. Many of the techniques (e.g., firearms and hand-to-hand self-defense) taught in most personal security courses are useful only in the counter phase – the phase that comes only after the attempts to avoid and evade have failed.

A number of studies have shown the value of problem solving based on intuition rather than detailed analysis. The book *Blink* by Malcolm Gladwell gives excellent examples of incidents in which people respond appropriately in the "blink of an eye." The counter argument is presented in *Think* by Michael R. LeGault. In fact, both authors have a point. For our purposes it seems reasonable to conclude that there are situations in which extensive and detailed analysis is appropriate. This approach would apply when you are evaluating the most likely threats that you might encounter in a given environment. Once that threat has presented itself, you must react intuitively – not analyze.

If we accept the definition of intuition as, "...the way we translate our experiences into judgments and decisions by using patterns to recognize what's going on in a situation and to recognize the typical action script with which to react" (Klein, 2003, p. 23), relying on intuition makes perfect sense. In fact, in the few seconds in which we must react to a threat, what other tool could we possibly use? There is no time to conduct a detailed analysis of the problem and to compare the pros and cons of various solutions. Recent studies have shown that we are able to unconsciously use our intuition to react in a small fraction of the time it would take to consciously analyze a situation.

| React |

How then can we prepare to use our intuition? By creating the experiences that will form the basis of our judgments and decisions upon which we will rely when threatened. Those experiences may take the form of simulations of similar incidents, studies, training, or even simple visualizations. The more ingrained those experiences are, the more likely they will form that basis. Merely hearing or reading of a good response to a specific threat is not likely to be embedded sufficiently for us to expect it to be useful in guiding our response to that threat. The response must be fixed to the extent that it is automatic, habitual, and requires no conscious thought.

PRINCIPLES

Plan:
> Analyze the threat before the event.
> Analyze your situation from the enemy's perspective.
> Predict.
> Plan for 360 degree security.
> Prepare.
> Spend the greatest effort in preparation for the most likely scenarios.
> Anticipate.
> Visualize.
> Coordinate, but do not depend on others.

Practice.
Emphasize the basics.
Have alternatives.
Leave as many options open as possible

Keep it simple:
Employ gross motor skills.
Avoid skills requiring fine or complex motor skills.

Be unpredictable:
Vary modes of travel, routes, and/or times.
Make use of surprise and/or counter surprise.
Disrupt the attacker's plan.

Be observant:
Study your surroundings.
Know what is normal.
Scan.
Maintain a broad perspective.
Avoid distractions.
Never go from a secure area to a non-secure area without first checking out the non-secure area.

Trust your intuition:
Don't confirm the attack site (the X).
If you suspect an attack is about to occur at a certain place, do not go there.

Analyze before the attack – React to the attack:

If on the X – move.

Always have a safe haven:
Follow through.
Continue avoiding, evading, and/or countering until certain you are safe.

HABITS

Why are habits important? Most of the things we do are done without conscious thought. Imagine having to deliberate each time you put one foot in front of the other, or turn your head when someone shouts your name, or push the brake pedal to slow your car. The ability to rely on unconscious habits, along with intuition and heuristics, frees the conscious mind for other things.

Forming a new habit is accomplished by developing a neural pathway. A neural pathway is part of a complex of nerve cells which connects the brain with other parts of the body. When the brain sends impulses through this network to perform a given task, a chain of nerve cells establishes a circuit. Each time the same action is performed, the pathway is reinforced, and the action becomes more ingrained. Eventually the behavior becomes an unconscious habit. New habits are formed by modifying actions and by strengthening the resultant substitute neural pathways through repetition.

Habits can be good or bad - helpful or harmful. With sufficient effort, bad habits can be replaced with good ones. A major deterrent to easily breaking an established habit is that it is performed without thought. Each time it is performed the likelihood of its being thoughtlessly applied in the future increases. The fact that something is done without thinking is, by definition, what makes it a habit. In order to develop a new habit the existing routine has to be deliberately replaced with a new one and then repeated until a new neural pathway is created, strengthened, and internalized. The new practice then becomes the new unconsciously performed habit.

One particularly concerning habit is a natural lack of a sufficient awareness of our surroundings. Unless someone is consciously on alert because of some premonition, they are likely to be in a default, largely oblivious condition. Normally, this ignorance of all of the details of the environment is beneficial. It allows concentration without distraction. However, it can also blind a potential victim to very real dangers.

Many security specialists advise to constantly scan; to "keep your head on a swivel;" to be continuously aware of your surroundings. All of this is excellent advice but cliches are not effective tools for maintaining awareness. If we do not expect trouble, human nature induces us to default to a less vigilant condition. When we do not anticipate danger, we tend not to notice it until it is too late to respond effectively.

Unless they are distracted, people habitually look where they are going. They do this unconsciously. Even though they are looking, they can still be surprised if they do not have a framework to analyze what is happening around them. To be aware, looking is not enough. You must be looking *for* something. You must have a strategy to determine what you are looking for and a way to turn "seeing" into true awareness. Methods for improving this awareness are covered in the chapters on OBSERVATION SKILLS, COMMENTARY DRIVING, and AWARENESS AND ANALYSIS.

According to Charles Duhigg in *The Power of Habit: Why We Do What We Do In Life And Business,* developing a new habit requires three things: a cue (or reminder), a routine, and a reward. The routine must be frequently repeated until it becomes "hard wired."

DEVELOPING HABITS (the four Rs)

REMINDER
ROUTINE
REWARD
REPETITION

You have developed the habit of looking both ways before crossing the street or you would probably not have survived to be reading this. You do it without thinking. In the United States you probably look to the left and then to the right and then to the left again. You make that final check to the left because the most immediate potential threat will come from that direction (since vehicle traffic is on their right side of the road - your left). This habit was created by using a cue (reaching an intersection), a routine (looking both ways), and a reward (avoiding an accident).

If we know in advance that there will be a threat at a certain time and place, we will either not go there at that time or, if the risk cannot be avoided, we will at least be on guard. We are observant when crossing the street because we know that it is potentially dangerous. It is when we are not aware of potential danger that we are inattentive. The safer the feeling, the more complacent the attitude, the more shocking and debilitating the effect of sudden surprise.

When they are surprised, humans involuntarily freeze as they attempt to evaluate their situation and decide what to do. This temporary inaction is the purpose of the criminal or terrorist's use of surprise. If we are paralyzed by surprise before even recognizing what particular danger we face, self-defense techniques will be useless. If we have anticipated possible threats, we can react immediately with a planned response.

Soldiers on patrol, police responding to a call, and security personnel guarding a principal are alert. It is their job when they are "on" and their overriding focus is on situational awareness. When we (or they) are merely going about routine tasks, threats are probably far from conscious consideration and situational awareness is reduced.

There is ample available information covering the analysis of possible threat indicators such as inappropriate behavior or dress, body language, and micro expressions (brief involuntary facial indications of emotion). These analyses presume the indicator has been observed. A look of contempt means nothing if the person displaying that expression has not been noticed. Develop the habit of first examining and analyzing your environment and then looking for specific indicators. Too often we concentrate on the steps following the realization that there is an imminent threat and too little on the steps leading to that realization.

How can we use the four Rs to develop habits to improve our situational awareness?

THE REMINDERS

The difficult part of developing the awareness habit is remembering to practice it. Reminders to practice the routine that will eventually become a new habit are required. The new awareness habit should be practiced whenever the environment changes. Therefore, there should be as many reminders as possible.

When I first started experimenting with the technique described in the chapter on AWARENESS AND ANALYSIS, I found it both difficult to remember to do it and then to remember to keep doing it. The solution to my problem was to have prompts to frequently remind me of the need to observe and analyze the situation.

Using something yellow as a visual reminder is a helpful technique. Yellow tends to stand out against most backgrounds. Yellow traffic signs worldwide mean caution and can subliminally raise awareness. Another reason for choosing yellow as the color of your visual reminders will become obvious in the COLOR CODES chapter.

Place reminders where they will be noticed. In the case of commentary driving, placing a piece of yellow tape somewhere where it will be obvious can serve as a reminder. Putting a small piece of yellow tape somewhere on a global positioning system (GPS) device may work for you. Consider sticking a piece of yellow tape at the 12:00 o'clock position on the steering wheel. If your car requires removing the key from the ignition (as opposed to newer cars that allow the key to be kept in a pocket), placing something yellow on the key ring may help. Seeing the yellow item as you remove the keys from the car then serves as a reminder.

Thinking of appropriate places for reminders outside the vehicle may be more difficult. If you look at your cellphone frequently, placing a piece of yellow tape on the phone may be useful. (It may also remind you that you should be observing your environment, *not* staring at your phone.) Placing a cue at eye level on the inside of the door or door frame of your residence can remind you to be aware as you are about to enter the most statistically dangerous environment for a specifically targeted attack - near your residence, in the morning, on the way to work. It can also remind you to look through a window to study the environment you are about to enter while still in the relative safety of your home. (Never go from a secure area to a non-secure area without first checking out the non-secure area.) You can do something similar where you will be exiting your workplace. The more prompts you use the better.

THE ROUTINE (HABIT)

Habits which will increase awareness are discussed in detail in the chapters on OBSERVATION SKILLS, AWARENESS AND ANALYSIS, and COMMENTARY DRIVING.

THE REWARD

The reward for being observant is obvious - an awareness of things that you would not have noticed otherwise. The penalty for failure to observe is also obvious. At best you will be surprised when something unforeseen but non-threatening happens. At worst you will be stunned into passivity by an accident, crime, or physical attack.

REPETITION

"We are what we repeatedly do.
Excellence, then, is not an act, but a habit."
Aristotle

It is only through repetition that old neural pathways can be replaced with new ones. The more habits are practiced, the more skillfully the routine will be executed, and the safer you will be.

Developing a habit which will be performed unconsciously requires conscious effort. Implementing any new habit will be difficult at first. As in refining any new skill, the only way to improve is to practice. At the risk of being repetitive, you *must* practice observing and analyzing. Practice in relatively safe places and situations. You will then have properly developed the habit and will eventually employ it intuitively.

THE ATTACK CYCLE

There are numerous models of the methodology used by those who attack others. All criminals, including terrorists, use a similar procedure. For our purposes, we will look at the "attack cycle" specifically as it applies to an attack against personnel. The same model can be and is used in planning and executing attacks against facilities.

The attack cycle can be expanded or contracted into any number of steps. For our purposes we will use a seven step model. In abbreviated form, the model is:

> ## THE ATTACK CYCLE
> **1. Initial list.**
> 2. Information collection (surveillance).
> 3. Target selection.
> 4. Information collection (surveillance).
> 5. Planning/rehearsal.
> 6. Event.
> 7. Escape.

1. **Initial list**. The initial list of possible targets is dictated by the assailants' objectives. It may include a very large group such as any official of a specific government, anyone of a given nationality, or, in the case of some terrorists, anyone at all. Recent events have shown that any American is a potential target.

31

Assuming that attacking the entire group is impractical, the assailants will narrow the field. For a target of opportunity criminal attack, the initial list may include anyone who happens by a street-corner thug.

```
THE ATTACK CYCLE
    1. Initial list.
    2. Information collection
    (surveillance).
    3. Target selection.
    4. Information collection
    (surveillance).
    5. Planning/rehearsal.
    6. Event.
    7. Escape.
```

2. **Information collection (including surveillance)**. The assailants will normally gather as much pertinent information as possible about members of the selected group. This may include information from open (readily available, often published) sources such as newspapers, registries, directories, social media, etc. The physical surveillance at this point may be the easiest to detect since it is often conducted by amateurs. In fact, those conducting the surveillance may have no idea that they are part of anything sinister. They may simply be providing times that a person included in the initial list passes a given point. In the target of opportunity example, the criminal may be studying everyone who passes by.

THE ATTACK CYCLE
1. Initial list.
2. Information collection (surveillance).
3. Target selection.
4. Information collection (surveillance).
5. Planning/rehearsal.
6. Event.
7. Escape.

3. **Target selection**. Once the data is collected, it is analyzed in an effort to narrow the possibilities. An unpredictable potential target may be rejected in favor of a more predictable one. Often terrorists and other criminals have eliminated someone from consideration because of some actual or perceived precaution that the target seems to take. However, the terrorist may select someone perceived to be important or high profile regardless of the precautions taken. Criminals may simply target someone who has something the criminal wants and who seems vulnerable enough that the criminal can get it.

```
THE ATTACK CYCLE
   1.  Initial list.
   2.  Information collection
   (surveillance).
   3.  Target selection.
   4.  Information collection
   (surveillance).
   5.  Planning/rehearsal.
   6.  Event.
   7.  Escape.
```

4. Information collection (including surveillance).
Information collection is now focused on the intended
target. Again, this may include information from open
sources. If, for example, the itinerary of a targeted
official is published, it makes much of the information
collection task easy for the would-be attacker.
(Examples include the assassination of President
Kennedy and the attempted assassinations of
Presidents Ford and Reagan and Pope John Paul II.)
In fact, it may make it unnecessary for the attacker to
surveil prior to the assault. However, in most cases
the assailant(s) will conduct some sort of surveillance
of the intended target.   Surveillance may now be
more difficult to detect than was the case in step 2
since it is more likely to be conducted by more
competent surveillants or by the actual assailants. In
the case of the target of opportunity crime, the
criminal will be making a more detailed assessment
of the selected victim.

```
THE ATTACK CYCLE
    1. Initial list.
    2. Information collection
    (surveillance).
    3. Target selection.
    4. Information collection
    (surveillance).
    5. Planning/rehearsal.
    6. Event.
    7. Escape.
```

5. Planning/rehearsal. Having selected their target, the assailants will plan their attack. They may or may not rehearse the actual assault. The target may play a role in the rehearsal. Often surviving victims will say something like, "The same thing happened to me a week before the attack." This was probably a rehearsal carried up to the point just short of the final assault. In the criminal scenario the attacker will be formulating a plan or re-thinking a previously devised plan.

In the case of the well-planned terrorist attack, these first five steps may take weeks, months, or even years. In the case of the street thug, these first five steps may take place in a matter of seconds.

```
┌─────────────────────────────────────┐
│           THE ATTACK CYCLE           │
│         1.  Initial list.            │
│         2.  Information collection    │
│         (surveillance).              │
│         3.  Target selection.        │
│         4.  Information collection    │
│         (surveillance).              │
│         5.  Planning/rehearsal.      │
│         6.  Event.                   │
│         7.  Escape.                  │
│                                      │
└─────────────────────────────────────┘
```

6.   **Event**.   In the terrorist scenario, the assailant arrives at the time and place of his choosing. This, of course, implies that the assailants can predict when an appropriate victim will be at a given site.   This ability to predict becomes an important consideration. (In fact, denying the terrorist the ability to predict where you will be at any given time is critical to your personal security.   We will revisit this repeatedly in the chapters to follow.) With the assailants in place, the victim arrives. Often the assailants will employ surveillance again to ensure that they have the right target before launching the assault. Statistically, a target who has gotten to this stage without recognizing that he is targeted has less than a one in ten chance of successfully avoiding, evading, or countering, the attack.

THE ATTACK CYCLE
1. Initial list.
2. Information collection (surveillance).
3. Target selection.
4. Information collection (surveillance).
5. Planning/rehearsal.
6. Event.
7. Escape.

7. **Escape**. Assuming that the assailants are not suicidal, they will attempt to escape.

This cycle is important to us because it points out where, when, and how we can discover that we are targeted for attack.

THE ATTACK CYCLE
1. Initial list.
2. Information collection (surveillance).
3. Target selection.
4. Information collection (surveillance).
5. Planning/rehearsal.
6. Event.
7. Escape.

It is very unlikely that we will learn that we are the targets of a possible attack during stages 1, 3, or 5. These processes can be carried out with the plotters hidden from our view. During the surveillance phases of steps 2 and 4 it is possible that we may see the surveillants. It is also possible that we will see a rehearsal in step 5 *if* we are a part of that rehearsal. Assuming step 6 takes longer than an instant, we may see the final assault developing but it may well be too late to respond appropriately by then. The problem will normally be that, even though we may see the surveillance, we might not recognize it as surveillance. Surveillance is normally disguised to look like anything but what it actually is. Another problem is that we must somehow differentiate between activities that might be long-term surveillance and those activities that may be the brief surveillance that is the precursor to an imminent attack. These will be addressed in the chapter on SURVEILLANCE DETECTION.

THE COLOR CODES

Many security experts advocate the use of colors to describe various levels of awareness. The code, proposed by Colonel Jeff Cooper, can be very helpful if it reminds you to be appropriately alert. We find it particularly helpful to relate the alert conditions to the heart rate and its corresponding physiological effects. The code is described below:

WHITE (60 to 80 beats per minute)

This is a **normal**, non-combative state of mind. When in condition white you are totally unaware of your surroundings. There is no perceived threat. There is nothing inherently wrong with condition white. If you have secured your home and are asleep in bed you are in condition white. In fact, you will destroy your mental health, and probably your physical health as well, if you constantly force yourself to be too anxious. If used inappropriately, however, condition white is the victim's state of mind. Condition white corresponds to the normal resting heart rate of 60 to 80 beats a minute.

YELLOW (still 60 to 80 beats per minute)

This is a state of **relaxed alertness**. You are generally conscious of your surroundings. It is the condition that you should be in whenever you are in unsecured or public places. Going to condition yellow is probably the most important consideration of the color codes. Going into the other conditions will be fairly automatic. In yellow you are still relaxed but alert. You will be observing and questioning your surroundings, but have a normal heart rate and suffer no ill effects.

ORANGE (115 to 145 beats per minute)

This is a state of **alarm**. You are specifically conscious of your surroundings. There is a perceived threat but you need more information in order to deal with it. In condition orange you will begin to lose fine motor skills and may begin to suffer from a number of other symptoms. You will, however, be at your maximum performance level in the areas of complex motor skills, visual reaction time, and cognitive reaction time.

RED (155 beats per minute and higher)

There is a **confrontation in progress**. Your heart rate increases to between 175 and 190 beats a minute. Your mental processing begins to shut down. You have lost your fine motor skills and are now losing your complex motor skills. Gross motor skills increase. You experience tunnel vision, loss of depth perception, and experience auditory exclusion. You may freeze in fright. Since your ability to think will be limited, whatever response you are going to execute will be the result of previous planning, rehearsal, habit, training, visualization, and/or practice.

BLACK (shock)

Recently it has become popular in the security community to include condition black. It refers to shock and implies the **inability to do anything** to save yourself. If you are surprised into condition black, and then repeatedly receive additional jolts, you may remain in shock for a very long time (perhaps the rest of your life).

As one expert has put it, "You can survive excitement. Surprise will kill you." Going from condition white through yellow to orange to red will prepare you for the fight (or flight) of your life. Going directly from condition white to black can leave you a quivering mass of useless flesh. Compare your body's reaction in two situations. In the first you are driving and see a warning sign that there is a stop light ahead. A little farther down the road you see the light, which has just turned yellow – warning you that it is about to turn red. Finally, it turns red and you bring your vehicle to a stop. In the second situation you are casually driving when your passenger suddenly screams, "STOP!" Your reaction will certainly be different. Your reaction in the first case will probably be more effective than in the second. Unfortunately, you will not see signs reading,

41

"Ambush Ahead." Our task is to identify the signs that you will see – if you are looking.

Have you ever driven somewhere and, once you arrived at your destination, realized that you had no memory of having driven there? You were in condition white. In this condition you will not notice the subtle indicators of trouble.

To be sufficiently aware of your surroundings you must be in condition yellow. Assuming you are not paranoid or suffer from some other psychological problem, you will be relaxed, so stress need not be a particular concern. You can relax and still be aware of what is going on around you. It is important as you observe your surroundings to determine what is "normal." Only then will you recognize the abnormal – those signs which indicate you are being watched or that an attack is imminent.

Condition yellow is the most critical because it is the one that requires a conscious effort. Once you are in condition orange or red, you do not need a reminder to remain alert. In condition red you will be on autopilot.

See the chapters on HABITS, OBSERVATION SKILLS, AWARENESS AND ANALYSIS, and COMMENTARY DRIVING for recommendations for getting into and maintaining condition yellow.

ROUTE ANALYSIS

"If you don't know where you are going, you'll end up someplace else."

Yogi Berra

While you may be susceptible to a random "target of opportunity" attack at other times, a deliberate attack targeted specifically against you is most likely to occur at some time and place where your presence has been predicted by the attackers. Statistically, you are most likely to be attacked during your routine (frequently repeated) travel. By analyzing your own routine, it is possible to predict with some degree of accuracy where and when you are most vulnerable to attack. Knowing this, you can determine how you should plan to avoid, or to evade, or where to go after countering such an attack. Routine trips are critical because they are predictable. Assuming that they are not publicized, non-routine trips, by definition, are unpredictable.

Studies of planned attacks against individuals show that more than four out of every five such attacks take place when the target of the attack is in or near a vehicle. Four out of every five attacks also occur in the morning, near the residence, as the target departs for work. Three out of every four such attacks will fit both profiles – in or near a vehicle, in the morning, near the home, on the way to work.

> Statistically, you are most likely to be attacked in the morning.
> Near your residence.
> On the way to work.

This is because:

1. You are generally more predictable in the morning than at the end of the day.

2. Traveling to and from work is the most routine pattern for most of us.

3. Your residence is an area of mandatory and, therefore, predictable travel.

4. There is generally less security around your residence than around your workplace.

The purpose of route analysis is not to find the perfect route. Since the start point and destination of routine travel routes are predictable, there is no such thing as the perfect route. If you repeat the "best" route too often it becomes the worst possible route. Instead, you should analyze as many route variations as possible in order to determine the advantages and disadvantages of each. Each route will have critical areas where you must exercise increased caution.

You must vary routes as much as possible. However, some routes are so fraught with danger that you should never use them. If the route is overwhelmingly advantageous to the attackers, and if you use it even infrequently, the attackers may choose to set up there and wait for that occasion when you decide to take it. Although we treat the varying of routes as a principle, we do not mean to imply that the principle should override common sense.

Some routes should *never* be used.

You should also consider whether you are a specific target or if the would-be attackers would be satisfied targeting anyone who fits a profile similar to yours. If they would attack anyone with your general profile, you must also ensure that your route avoids patterns established by other possible targets.

AREAS OF MANDATORY AND PREDICTABLE TRAVEL

Any route includes two places where you must be – your start point and your destination. These are the minimum areas of mandatory travel for any trip.

A given trip may have other areas which you must traverse. For example, if there is a river between your start point and your destination and only one bridge across it, that bridge becomes another area of mandatory travel. If there is only one route from your start point to your destination, the entire route is an area of mandatory travel.

Areas of predictable travel include areas of mandatory travel plus any other areas which you routinely pass through. If you choose to travel the same route each time you make a particular trip, the entire route is predictable. You have given your potential attacker the entire route from which to pick surveillance and attack sites.

> Predictability = Vulnerability

Where you are predictable you are vulnerable. You cannot avoid the areas of mandatory travel. However, as much as possible, limit your predictability to only those places where you have no choice. Vary the times you will use these predictable areas. If possible, vary the mode of transportation. These areas should always be considered to be critical parts of your travel. You should always take the appropriate precautions discussed elsewhere in this book as you travel through these areas.

> VARY the **time**.
> VARY the **route**.
> VARY the **mode**.

Route analysis includes the following steps. These steps must be followed for every routine trip. These may include work, scheduled events, appointments, entertainment, shopping, stopping for gas, picking the kids up from or driving them to school, etc.

1. Obtain as many various types of maps as possible covering all logical routes. It is important to try to obtain a variety of maps because different maps may include different features. Some may show specific locations of potential safe havens such as hospitals, police and fire stations, etc. Others may show topography, one-way streets, bridges, or other helpful information. Internet-based programs such as Google Earth can provide additional information.

2. Mark all logical routes from start to finish for each travel requirement. Include all alternate routes. Keep all route information secured. It must not fall into the hands of would-be assailants.

3. Mark all known areas/points of interest from the list below. (Some of these may be refined based on the follow-on ground reconnaissance.)

4. Conduct ground reconnaissances to confirm, refute, and/or add to the information found in the map study. While these surveys are most helpful if conducted at various times and days and under various weather conditions, ensure that you include the general time that you are most likely to be using the route.

5.   Record observations based on the map and reconnaissance studies.

6. Update the analysis each time you use the route or a portion of the route

ROUTE ANALYSIS INCLUDES DETERMINING:

Possible routes.

Areas of mandatory travel.

Areas of predictable travel.

Safe havens. (See below.)

Medical facilities (if not already addressed as safe havens).

Police and other security force locations (if not already addressed as safe havens).

Areas where movement is canalized.

Probable surveillance sites. (See below.)

Probable attack sites. (See below.)

Traffic patterns (including at various times/ days).

Alternate routes.

Route analysis is a continuing process. Update the analysis each time you use a route.

SAFE HAVENS

A safe haven is any place where you can find refuge from an attacker. It is a place the attacker is likely to avoid. It may be a police station, a guarded facility, or simply a crowded place. Some terrorism specialists suggest first finding the potential safe havens and only then determining routes based on the availability of safe havens on or near those routes.

The question of what may serve as a suitable safe haven depends, in part, on the primary threat. For example, if the primary threat is from a terrorist organization which attacks a specific target and avoids collateral damage, a crowded area may serve as a safe haven. If, on the other hand, the local terrorists are interested in causing as much damage as possible and do not concern themselves with collateral damage, crowded areas should be avoided.

PROBABLE SURVEILLANCE SITES

A probable static surveillance site will have the following characteristics:

CHARACTERISTICS OF STATIC SURVEILLANCE SITES

1.   Located in or near the target's area of predictable travel.
2.   Offers a view of the target of the surveillance.
3.   Allows or provides either an obvious and innocent explanation for the surveillant's presence or the capability for the surveillant to hide from the view of the target.

PROBABLE ATTACK SITES

A probable attack site will have the following characteristics:

CHARACTERISTICS OF ATTACK SITES

1.   Located in or near the target's area of predictable travel.

2.   Allows or provides either an obvious and innocent explanation for the attacker(s)' presence or the capability for the attacker(s) to hide from the view of the target.

3. Offers a means to control the target long enough to achieve the objective of the attack.

4. Provides one or more routes of escape for the attacker (not required in the case of suicide attacks).

ROLE REVERSAL

Imagine that you are the terrorist. Using the criteria above, find those places where you would conduct surveillance on your routes. Find those places where you would attack. Since using these criteria for determining the best possible location(s) (from the attackers' point of view) is exactly what the attacker will be doing, the sites you select will very likely match those chosen by your opponent.

OBSERVATION SKILLS

Observation expertise, like the other skills discussed here, must be practiced frequently to be of any value. If you have not developed the habit of observing the normal, how can you expect to recognize the abnormal? Observing can be made a habit. For observation to be made habitual requires a great deal of concentration and effort in the beginning and frequent revisiting to ensure that the practice is continuing. Observing includes a number of steps: sensing, perceiving, remembering, and acting or reacting.

SENSING

"You can observe a lot just by watching."
Yogi Berra

In order to observe something we must first sense it. It is obvious that if we do not see, hear, feel, taste, or smell something we cannot "observe" it. The first step in observing then is to sense what is happening by remaining alert, scanning our surroundings, and avoiding distractions. Too often we fail to sense what is going on around us because we are not aware of our surroundings or are distracted by something insignificant.

DISTRACTIONS

Position - We tend to focus on the center of our view rather than the periphery.

Color - The brighter the color the greater the tendency to be distracted.

Sound - When we search for a specific street sign or address, we routinely turn the car radio down or off without thinking about it.

Contrast - We tend to stare at what stands out.

Movement - We are drawn to the dynamic versus the static.

PERCEIVING

"You see, but you do not observe.
The distinction is clear."

Sherlock Holmes
A Scandal in Bohemia

Although we may sense exactly the same information as others, we may have very different perceptions of its meaning.   We are all subject to biases that influence our perceptions.   We tend to try to explain to ourselves, either consciously or unconsciously, what we see around us.   Other problems related to cognitive bias are discussed below.

REMEMBERING

Everything that we see, hear, feel, taste, or smell goes into our flash memory.   That information (actually our perception of what we have sensed) will generally remain for approximately six to eight seconds before we unconsciously eliminate that information (forget it) and replace it with new data. The information which we determine (either consciously or unconsciously) is important to us will be kept and filed in our short term memory and will remain for between two and 48 hours when again it will be eliminated (forgotten) or retained for continuing or future use.   If we determine that we need the information (again either consciously or unconsciously) we will retain it, perhaps forever, by transferring it to our long term memory.

As you drive you must occasionally stop for a red light.   If you stop and look in your rear view mirror and see a car behind you, it will register in your flash memory. If that car was approaching at a speed that made you unsure that it would be able to stop before hitting your car, the scene will be filed in your short term memory.   If the car stops in time you will probably soon forget the incident.   If, however, that car does not stop and in hitting your car does serious damage and injures you, the same information that you gathered from that initial glance in your mirror may remain for a lifetime.

ACTING/REACTING

Improving observation will be meaningless if you do not also improve the action or reaction that you take in response to your observations. Without preparation you are likely to do little or nothing when faced with a life-threatening attack.

IMPROVING OBSERVATION

Unfortunately, many of us seem unable to remember even those things which we have consciously determined to be important. We must improve both our observation and memory skills.

Perhaps the best way to improve observation skills is to have an objective in mind. It is much easier to notice the thing that you are looking for than somehow picking out the most important thing in an amorphous array of distractions.

No one can be thoroughly observant all the time. Although you should stay alert (condition yellow) whenever you are on the street, you should make a concentrated effort to observe in and around critical areas. These will include those areas discussed in the previous chapter on ROUTE ANALYSIS.

```
┌─────────────────────────────────────────────┐
│          BE PARTICULARLY OBSERVANT            │
│            (Be in condition yellow)           │
│                                               │
│  In areas of mandatory and predictable travel.│
│  Around potential safe havens.                │
│  In areas where your movement is canalized.   │
│  At possible surveillance sites.              │
│  At probable attack sites.                    │
└─────────────────────────────────────────────┘
```

If you conscientiously study these places each time you travel you will eventually develop the kind of expertise Malcolm Gladwell discusses in his excellent book, *Blink: The Power of Thinking Without Thinking*. When you have developed this knowledge you will be able to discover at a glance when something has changed. You may not be able to immediately say what it is, but you will realize that something is different.   You may ascribe your feelings to extra sensory perception or a sixth sense but they are actually the result of the expertise you have gained about what is normal. If you are able to recognize that something is "wrong" (abnormal) and you take some action to avoid a threat because you feel that something is not right, that is good enough. You now have the rest of your life to figure out why you had that feeling. Gavin de Becker essentially argued for acting on this feeling in his *The Gift of Fear: Survival Signals That Protect Us From Violence*.

GENERAL GUIDANCE FOR OBSERVING

Be in condition yellow.

Search systematically.

Use the same technique each time you observe a specific object (top to bottom or bottom to top, left to right or right to left, etc.)

Do not fixate on one object or one part of a scene.

If possible, view an object from different angles.

Include the periphery.

Compare unknown items with known items.

Take in overall shapes.

Use tagging (a descriptive nickname) to remember what you have seen.

Be aware of cognitive bias.

CONFIRMATION BIAS

A major obstacle to good observation is confirmation bias – the tendency to see what we want or expect to see. Motorcyclists are familiar with this problem. Most people driving cars, vans, or trucks are looking for other large vehicles, not motorcycles. Therefore the drivers of larger vehicles may pull out directly in front of a motorcycle and later claim that they did not see it. They saw that motorcycle but it did not register because of their confirmation bias.

The mind has an amazing ability to fill in blanks to make everything appear logical. In one video exercise we often use in training, viewers are shown a man sitting at a desk with a number of distractions on the desk and on the wall beyond. There is no sound with the video. After a few seconds the man looks up and gets up from the desk, walking out of the camera's view. We immediately see a scene in a hallway with a man answering a phone. The students are well aware that there may be discrepancies in the two segments. When asked to say what they saw, students will almost always say that they saw a man get up from a desk and answer a phone. They will often catalog differences to include: the man's clothes have changed, he is wearing different glasses, he has combed his hair differently, etc. Few notice the real significant change between the two scenes. Although he looks somewhat similar, the man in the second scene is not the same person that appeared in the first one. When the students are told that they saw two different people and then see the scenes again, they immediately confirm that fact. In fact, the two scenes are completely unrelated. Viewers just assume the connection because the second scene is seen immediately after the first. The mind creates a connection because of confirmation bias. We expect a connection so we imagine one where none exists. (Simons, 2003.)

The example above illustrates the human tendency to rationalize. If violent attacks are not a part of your everyday life, when you are subjected to such an attack you may immediately (and unconsciously) attempt to find an explanation that more closely approximates your normal experiences. Often when debriefed after an attack, a victim will say, "I couldn't believe it," or "I couldn't believe it was happening to me." In one case, a witness to an ambush in which two people were killed and several others were wounded assumed that he was seeing actors making a movie. Apparently the fact that there were no cameras or crews present was unconsciously dismissed in order to fit the perception. We naturally try to make everything fit into our preconceived ideas about how things should be. We often make assumptions not supported by the evidence.

As mentioned earlier, distractions significantly limit our ability to observe and understand what we see. Distractions may be based on size, color, shape, shine, noise, smell, or any of a number of other factors.

For example, I returned home from work along the same country road for several weeks. About a mile from my house I passed a mailbox painted a very bright red. By the time I saw the mailbox I was usually tired and eager to get home. I realized after at least five trips that as soon as the mailbox came into view I would focus on it until I had passed it. There was no particular reason for staring other than the fact that the bright color caught my rather absentminded attention. When I finally realized that I had been completely distracted by the red mailbox, it occurred to me that there was no reason for a mailbox to be there. I had not seen a nearby house or even a driveway that might have led to a house. There was nothing but fields and woods. It was only the next time I went by that I finally realized that there were two conspicuous houses, one on either side of the road with driveways leading to each one. Every time I had passed by I had been so distracted by the mailbox that I failed to notice them.

MULTITASKING

Numerous recent studies have found that multitasking (accomplishing two or more tasks simultaneously) is not practicable. When we think we are multitasking we are actually "switch tasking," concentrating first on one task then quickly switching our focus to another. These studies show that accomplishing two simple tasks can each take twice as long when we attempt to multitask.

In later AWARENESS AND ANALYSIS and COMMENTARY DRIVING chapters we advise focusing on a number of objects - but in succession - not at the same time.

AWARENESS AND ANALYSIS

Most personal security texts and courses concentrate almost entirely on responses to an identified threat - running away from it, hiding from it, or, most often, combating it. High speed driving, martial arts, and marksmanship are useful skills - but only after you are aware that there is a threat.

Having realized that there is a possible threat, you must then identify the nature of that threat in order to formulate and execute an appropriate response. That takes time. The earlier you observe possible danger, the more time you have available. In a sudden unexpected and violent attack you will be denied that advantage. Surprise is the criminal and terrorist's most powerful weapon; it is the victim's greatest vulnerability.

A technique to counter this problem while driving is explained in the COMMENTARY DRIVING chapter. Commentary driving forces awareness by requiring a driver to talk to himself out loud. Although "commentary walking," "commentary standing around," or "commentary sitting" would effectively keep us alert at other times, talking to ourselves in public would draw unwanted attention and be disquieting to others. When not in a vehicle, we need a way to stimulate awareness and analysis that does not require verbalization.

63

One approach (known as "Kim's game" from Rudyard Kipling's novel *Kim*) is to view a scene for a limited time and then look away and describe as many details as possible. A flaw in this type of training is that it encourages indiscriminate observation. An exercise in which someone scans a room and is later tested with questions such as whether the pattern in the curtains was geometric or floral or how many tea cups were in the china cabinet is counterproductive. Part of the genius of the brain is that it employs selective attention, discarding the irrelevant to allow it to focus on critical issues. To concentrate on and quickly analyze important things (in this case, dangers), you *must* ignore the irrelevant. Situational awareness practice should not emphasize more observations but more *deliberate* and *discerning* observations leading to an accurate perception of the threat.

As stated earlier, telling ourselves to maintain awareness is ineffective. To focus on irrelevant details is both ineffective and distracting. We must not only sense what is going on around us, we must know what we are looking for and what it might mean. In order to ensure that we know what is important, a checklist of critical information is invaluable.

Going through the thought process described below may seem contrived and frivolous at first. However, you will be doing it all in your mind and no one else need be aware of it. The procedure costs nothing and could save your life. Several suggested reminders to practice the technique were covered in the HABITS chapter.

When entering a new environment, think through the following checklist using the acronym "ESCAPE" or "ESCAPED." Simply thinking of the word may psychologically prime you for what is likely to be the most advantageous action available - escape. It will also force you into alert condition yellow (relaxed awareness). Analyzing each component will help identify threats and possible courses of action. At first it might help to carry a small card with the acronym and the word or words represented by each letter. Refer to it as you enter each new environment until you have memorized it.

ESCAPE(D)

Environment
Scan
Cover and **C**oncealment
Allies
Potential threats
Entrances and **E**xits
Distance (optional)

Below are some considerations and questions as they apply to the components of the procedure. More detailed factors are listed than could reasonably be examined in each case. They are provided here to give an idea of the kind of matters you should consider and the sort of questions you should ask yourself.

Environment

Although generally surveying your surroundings may not be sufficient in itself to make you safe, it is a huge improvement over blindly stumbling around until something bad happens. This is a quick first impression which will be refined as the other considerations are examined.

What is your overall assessment of the environment? Is it generally friendly or hostile? Is it confined or expansive? Is it crowded or deserted? Is it bustling or calm? Is activity spread throughout the area or are there pockets of more intense activity? Can you see the entire environment or should you move to be able to observe more of it? Is the area well or poorly lit? Are you well or poorly protected? Is it a "gun-free" zone? If so, will this make the environment more or less dangerous? Are there any obvious distractions? If so, is everyone in the environment paying attention to the distraction or are some ignoring it?

Analyzing the general environment will force you to apply the next step - scanning.

Scan

As you scan, refine your analysis of your surroundings. Investigate the issues outlined by the ESCAPE(D) mnemonic. Scanning will maximize the advantages of both foveal vision (the approximately one degree of vision in the center of the eye where color and detail are clear) and peripheral vision (the approximately 170 degrees of monochromatic unclear vision in the periphery of the eye which is particularly adept at perceiving movement).

All other considerations being equal, the closest threat is the most dangerous. Therefore, when indoors or on foot, start from close-in and scan from side to side to as far as you can see. However, when you are near vehicular traffic which can close on you rapidly, start your scan from the farthest distance you can see and scan toward your current position. Do not ignore higher elevations (buildings, balconies, overpasses, hills, etc.). When the entire observable area has been scanned, repeat the process. Do not just move your eyes from side to side. Actually think about what you are seeing by looking for the issues outlined in the ESCAPE(D) mnemonic.

Tunnel vision is a natural reaction to noticing a possible threat. Do not fixate on one thing. With tunnel vision you are using only that one percent of your field of view that foveal vision provides. What you see may be a distraction, something less menacing than other potential threats, or only one component of a much larger danger. If you determine it is the primary or only threat you can quickly return to it. Continue to search the entire area. Repetitive scanning is especially important if you are moving, since new areas for analysis will be exposed to view. Repetition is also critical in order to discover any changes in the environment.

Cover and Concealment

In this case cover is defined as protection from small arms fire or, possibly, vehicular assault. Concealment provides protection from being seen. An object may provide concealment but not cover. For example a plasterboard wall may hide you from observation (provides concealment) but will not stop a bullet (provides no cover). Moving from cover to cover may be preferable to making an exposed straight-line dash to the exit. Consider the advantages and disadvantages of cover or concealment versus increasing your distance from the threat.

What objects in the environment provide cover? What provides concealment? Where can you hide? If you are going to hide, is the ring tone on your cellphone muted? Is there a viable route from your present position to the cover or concealment? If you elect to hide, what options are available if you are discovered? If you use cover or concealment, how will it affect your ultimate escape? If the available cover or concealment provides only temporary safety, is it preferable to use it or to immediately exit the area?

Allies

Are you alone or with others? Is there anyone you should or must help? Where will you meet with others in your group once out of the immediate area? Have you established a rendezvous site and time? Is there anyone who might help you? If assaulting the attacker(s) en masse is a viable way to save lives, is it possible to sufficiently organize others? Are there police, security personnel or other first responders nearby? Can you get to them quickly? How can you communicate with them if they are not in the immediate area? Is there a way to communicate with others who might help you or who you need to help? Where is your phone? Do you have emergency services numbers on speed dial?

Potential threats

Look at people's hands; that is where an attacker is most likely to have a weapon.

What is the most likely threat? What could you do if such a threat materialized? How can you best avoid, evade, or counter the threat? What other dangers can you imagine? Who or what poses a threat?

Does anyone appear furtive, nervous, or tense? Who or what seems out of place or unnatural? Is anyone showing unusual interest in you? Is anyone acting significantly differently than others? Is anyone inappropriately dressed for the season, time, or area? Is anyone obviously trying to "look natural" or avoid eye contact with you? What is available to use to avoid, evade, or counter the threat? Is assaulting the threat either singly or en masse the best or only way to save lives?

Entrances and Exits

To the extent possible, keep the entrances in sight. As a general rule it is best to position yourself with your back against a wall facing the entrance. However, if this places you in a corner, far from any exits, you have sacrificed the ability to escape quickly for the ability to spot a threat quickly. Keep both concerns in mind in deciding where to stand or sit.

From where is an outside threat likely to come? Where are the exits and escape routes? Where can you go? How can you escape? Where can you position yourself to expedite your exiting the area if a threat appears? Does keeping the entrance in sight restrict your view of the rest of the environment? How would you get to an exit if the lights were turned off? Are there additional potential threats covering the exits? Is there danger of a mass rush to the exits if an attack is initiated?

Distance (optional)

You may add the final keyword "distance" to emphasize that you should continue to move once you have evaded the immediate threat. Do not stop only to be enveloped in a widening danger area. Keep in mind that some terrorist attacks will have multiple threats. The initial attack may be used, in part, to draw additional first responders or onlookers to the area in order to attack them. Get as far from the threat as possible and continue moving away.

TURNING OFF SITUATIONAL AWARENESS

Even if you are going to purposely "turn off" your situational awareness the checklist should be used.

For example, you get on an airplane for a very long flight, knowing you will need to sleep for at least part of the flight. Conduct an ESCAPE(D) analysis both in the airport departure area and again on the plane. If you have a confirmed assigned seat you can delay boarding to survey others as they board. Again analyze the ENVIRONMENT as you board the plane. SCAN as you approach your seat and then SCAN other passengers as they board. See what temporary COVER or CONCEALMENT, if any, is available. Identify potential ALLIES - the flight crew, others you are traveling with, etc. Attempt to identify POTENTIAL THREATS - anyone acting strangely or seeming out of place, for example. Find the nearest ENTRANCES/EXITS. Count the number of rows to the exits so that you can get out quickly, even if blinded by smoke and crawling on the floor. In a crash determine to get as much DISTANCE from the wreckage as possible as soon as possible. Listening to the flight attendant's briefing, reading the safety information card, and identifying the two nearest exits are the most important factors in determining who will survive a plane crash. In the event of a crash and fire, experts estimate that passengers will have 90 seconds to evacuate before they will be overcome by smoke.

The same type of analysis is used in a hotel room - another place you are going to purposely "turn off" your situational awareness as you sleep. From the moment you enter the lobby of the hotel, evaluate the ENVIRONMENT. SCAN all the areas of the hotel that you pass through or occupy. Identify possible COVER and CONCEALMENT both in your room and along the potential escape routes that you reconnoiter. Identify any ALLIES that you may rely on, or who may depend on you. Determine what POTENTIAL THREATS are present. Reconnoiter all possible ENTRANCES and EXITS. As in the case in an airplane, make sure that you can find exits even if blinded by smoke and crawling on the floor. Finally, collect all the items needed in an emergency evacuation and place them within immediate reach *before* going to sleep.

If you have conscientiously conducted the ESCAPE(D) procedure, you should be able to immediately and appropriately respond to an emergency that is initiated while you are not situationally aware (sleeping). You will be acting rather than wasting valuable time dazed, evaluating, and deciding.

The reward for employing the ESCAPE(D) habit quickly becomes apparent. You are keenly aware of what is going on around you and therefore able to analyze and evaluate your surroundings. You have the satisfaction of knowing that, if something untoward does happen, you will be prepared for it.

SURVEILLANCE DETECTION

It is critical that you develop the ability to detect surveillance in order to determine that you may be a target. We will examine two techniques of surveillance: following (or trailing) surveillance and static surveillance.

FOLLOWING SURVEILLANCE

Commonly people assume that surveillance means following someone. In fact, surveillants will follow someone to determine where he is going, what he is doing, or who he is meeting with. Police may follow a suspect for one or more of these reasons. Many organizations have adopted the techniques used to detect following surveillance and attempted to apply them to criminal and terrorist threat environments. This is dangerous.

Terrorists or criminals usually have no need to follow their intended victim and rarely use following surveillance. (They *may* choose to follow an intended victim to determine the target's routine. Rarely would they need to do so more than once.)

STATIC SURVEILLANCE

We will assume that terrorists have decided to attack you and that they know where you work. (Often the reason that they choose to attack you is based on your work.) As stated earlier, most attacks take place in the morning, near the residence, on the way to work. They can easily discover where you live by using static surveillance. The more predictable your route, the easier the surveillants' task. Prior to your arrival at work one morning they establish a perimeter around your office (a known point on your route). One member of the surveillance team sees you as you approach. Where you are first seen approaching establishes a second known point on your route to work. The next time the surveillants will set up on this new known point. They can continue in this manner until they have traced your entire route. Had we chosen an example in which the surveillants know were you live rather than where you work, they could use a similar technique to determine where you work.

In many cases, even this will not be necessary. Often they can determine where you live from readily available information. Westerners tend to stay in the same hotels. Your office may have apartments set aside for employees. The terrorists can stake out the hotels or apartments and pick from a variety of potential victims. They may infiltrate informants on the staff of your hotel, making surveillance even easier for them and more difficult for you to detect. In the past, some companies and government agencies published the routes and times they would provide employee transportation.   In these cases, surveillance was unnecessary.

```
┌─────────────────────────────────────────────┐
│ POSSIBLE INDICATORS OF SURVEILLANCE           │
│                                               │
│              LOCATION                         │
│            CORRELATION                        │
│             MISTAKES                          │
└─────────────────────────────────────────────┘
```

LOCATION

As stated in the ROUTE ANALYSIS chapter, a probable surveillance site has certain characteristics.

```
┌─────────────────────────────────────────────┐
│ CHARACTERISTICS OF STATIC SURVEILLANCE        │
│                  SITES                        │
│                                               │
│ 1.  Located in or near the target's area of   │
│ predictable travel.                           │
│ 2.  Offers a view of the target of the        │
│ surveillance.                                 │
│ 3.  Allows or provides either an obvious and  │
│ innocent explanation for the surveillant's    │
│ presence or the capability for the surveillant│
│ to hide from the view of the target.          │
└─────────────────────────────────────────────┘
```

There may be a number of people (any one of them could be a surveillant) at a possible surveillance site. For example, the site might be a bus stop. As you pass the bus stop you see a number of people, presumably waiting for a bus. In fact, they may all be doing exactly that. Or, one or more of them may be using the bus stop to disguise their real purpose. They may be there to observe your movements. It may seem difficult, if not impossible, to determine which, if any, of them are surveillants. You have already established several indicators. They are at the location that you predicted might be a surveillance site. It is near or in an area of predictable travel. It offers a view of your movement. It offers an obvious and innocent reason for a surveillant to be there.

CORRELATION AND MISTAKES

Once you have determined where the surveillance is likely to be, you can further refine your search. Let us assume that one of the people at the bus stop is, in fact, a surveillant. How can you determine that? One technique is to look for correlation – something that a suspect surveillant does that may be tied to what you are doing.

For example, as you drive past he may stare at you. He may check his watch. He might even jot a note. He could signal to an accomplice. He might leave the bus stop as soon as you pass without getting on a bus. In other words, he may do something that correlates to you or your activity. This would indicate that the supposed reason for his being there was a ruse – that the real reason was to surveil you.

Some analysts separate these possibilities into "correlation" and "mistakes." However, any of these could be considered both correlation and a mistake. Theoretically at least, a professional surveillant would not stare (correlation) or do any of the other things listed above, or be caught doing them (mistake). The true professional would get on a bus after you have passed. If someone leaves the bus stop without getting on a bus it exposes them as a possible surveillant. Terrorists and criminals are not always professional. The human tendency is to do just what is necessary.

In addition to varying your routes, you should also vary the time of your travel. What is a reasonable time for a person to wait at that particular bus stop? For the sake of discussion, let us assume that you have determined that buses going to all areas serviced by that particular stop arrive every 30 minutes. Seeing the same person at the bus stop on two days on which your passing varies by much more than 30 minutes should arouse your suspicion.

You have now established that a suspicious person is at the location where you could expect surveillance. You have also determined that the person does not have an obvious and innocent reason for being there – at least not at times more than 30 minutes apart.

One difficulty is that some or all of these indicators may occur out of your sight. In fact, the surveillant in our example could do all of the things mentioned (stare, check his watch, note, signal, and leave the site). Assuming he does it just after you have driven past, you may be unable to see any of it. The solution to this problem is counter surveillance. Enlist someone to watch the sites and people that you suspect may be surveillance. Instruct them to look for any correlation and/or mistakes.

In addition to varying your time and route of travel, you may be able to disrupt the surveillance effort by varying your mode of travel. You may be less predictable by driving your own car, carpooling, taking public transportation and/or driving someone else's car. However, a word of caution is in order. When you switch vehicles you inherit whatever patterns that vehicle may have established. You know where your own vehicle has been. There is no telling where someone else's has been. Are you unknowingly becoming the victim of an attack intended for someone else?

WHENEVER POSSIBLE, VARY:
1. The route…
2. The time…
3. The mode of travel.

If you are not sure whether you are seeing surveillance or the deployment of an attack team, immediately go to the nearest safe haven.

RECORD AND REPORT SUSPECTED SURVEILLANCE

If you detect surveillance, record it and report it. Do not let the surveillants know that you are aware of them. Doing so will result in their making significant changes. You may not see them again, but that does not mean that you have no surveillance. You should pay special attention to repeated sightings of the same people or vehicles. The greater the number of people in your workplace reporting such information, the greater the probability that you can identify the most likely surveillants. If several people are reporting sightings, be sure to check the latest information before each trip.

DRIVING BASICS

VEHICLE FAMILIARIZATION

Imagine the following situation. You are in a vehicle under attack. The vehicle has been disabled. It is dark. You fumble trying to get out of your seatbelt. You cannot find the handle to open the door. When you finally locate the door handle you realize that the handle alone will not open the door. You must first unlock the door with a separate device. Now you have to locate that device. You could die simply because you are not familiar with the vehicle.

KNOW YOUR VEHICLE.

Note that in the above example, the vehicle was under attack *and disabled*. We would remain In an operational vehicle, since it provides a means to avoid, evade, and even counter threats. An operational vehicle is a potent weapon.

Develop the habits that will ensure rapid familiarization. Every time you get into a vehicle immediately identify any differences between the vehicle you happen to be in and the vehicle(s) you are accustomed to.

CHANGING HABITS

The one thing that unites all human beings, regardless of age, gender, religion, economic status, or ethnic background, is that, deep down inside, we all believe that we are above average drivers.
Dave Barry, *Dave Barry Turns 50,*

Driving is rarely given the attention it deserves in personal security training. Too often instructors assume that we can drive fairly well. In fact, most of us do not drive nearly as well as we need to if we are to evade an attack.

Most of us learned to drive as teenagers. Some of the things we learned we have long since forgotten. In some cases we may have been taught things that, in a terrorist environment, are simply wrong. In any case, what you may or may not have been taught is irrelevant. What you do is critical. In an attack, if you do anything at all, you are likely to do what you habitually do as a result of a great deal of practice. At the time of an attack, the last thing you will be thinking about are basics like seat position, hand position, and proper use of the eyes. In fact, you should not be thinking about these things. You must do them properly without thinking.

In driving, as in most physical skills, it is important to emphasize the basics. Some people believe that, in a crisis, they will respond in the correct manner. They believe that they will be able to call on their intellect to overcome inappropriate habits – habits they have not bothered to reprogram. As mentioned in the introduction to this book, I have seen students driving right at the limit of adhesion for the first time in their lives, with their hearts racing, but with only one hand on the steering wheel. They knew better. They had just completed several days of training in high performance driving techniques. As they practiced the techniques at moderate speeds, none had attempted to drive with just one hand. But, under stress, their intellect was not a factor. When surprised, you will do what is habitual. Replacing old habits with new ones, especially after years of driving, takes several weeks of consistent practice. The basics should be practiced every time you drive.

Inspect the Vehicle.

Before opening the door of your vehicle you should always conduct an initial inspection. Depending on a number of factors, this may range from a long range examination to a fairly detailed and up close search for an improvised explosive device (IED). Vehicle search techniques will not be covered in detail here. If you suspect that an explosive may have been attached to your vehicle, immediately leave the area and notify the appropriate authorities.

Remember that a target of assassination is most vulnerable in the morning near the residence. If you are not in a secure location, balance that fact against the danger of using that time and place to inspect the vehicle.

Ensure that you have all items you will need in an emergency.

Start the Engine.

As soon as you have completed the inspection, start the engine. Even if you do not have enough time to accomplish the following steps, you will be able to move. None of the following procedures should take precedence over your ensuring that you can immediately move the vehicle.

Lock the Doors and Close the Windows.

Once in the vehicle, and assuming that there is not an immediate need to move, you should quickly ensure that all windows are closed and all doors are locked. Familiarize yourself with how to unlock the doors and exit quickly. Rehearse the process several times.

Adjust the Seat.

Make sure that the seat back is as vertical as practical. Leaning the seat back counters your ability to detect weight transfer while accelerating or slowing. Similarly, leaning to the side as you corner will decrease your ability to detect the transfer of weight resulting from cornering. Perhaps just as important, sitting up straight will significantly reduce fatigue and ensure a greater degree of alertness.

Position your buttocks well back into the seat. Maintain as much contact between the surface area of your body and the vehicle as possible. This will maximize sensations transmitted through the vehicle to your body, thus improving "communication" with the car. You should think of yourself as an extension of the vehicle. You receive inputs through your senses and transmit responses through your body to and through the mechanics of the vehicle to the tire contact patches. In essence, you are an integral part of the vehicle.

Move the seat far enough forward so that you could press the pedals all the way to the floorboard or firewall. You should be able to drape your wrist over the top of the steering wheel, with a slight bend in the elbow and without raising your shoulders off the back of the seat. This may place you closer to the wheel than you are used to. In some newer cars, the pedals can be adjusted to accommodate the length of the driver's legs. In this case, maximize the position of the torso and then adjust the pedals as required. Without this feature it may be necessary to compromise somewhat. With the introduction of air bags, many "experts" began advocating moving as far back as possible to avoid injury from a deploying air bag. Logic dictates that it would be preferable to avoid the collision in the first place. This can be done, in part, by maintaining the proper seating position.

If the vehicle has adjustable head restraints, place the top of the head restraint even with the top of your ears. This will ensure that the head restraint will do its job (restraining the head) in the event of a collision. If it is any lower the head restraint can act as a fulcrum, worsening whiplash in the event of an accident.

Fasten the Seat Belt.

The seat belt should be fastened in almost every case. Remember, you are statistically more likely to be involved in a traffic accident than to be the victim of an attack. The one exception to wearing the seat belt might be when you believe that the greatest risk you face at a particular time is someone placing an explosive charge on your vehicle. The response to this should be immediately getting out of the car and running as far and fast as possible. Once this is no longer the greatest threat (and it rarely is) you should refasten the seatbelt.

Properly Position Your Feet.

Your right foot should be placed on the brake so that, when the pedal is depressed as far as possible, the ball of the foot and toes are in contact with the pedal and the heel is resting on the floorboard. Place it far enough to the right side of the pedal so that you can release pressure on the brake and place the toes on the accelerator without raising your heel. Keeping your heel planted on the floorboard will allow you to rapidly pivot your foot to apply the brake in an emergency. This is much quicker than lifting the entire leg to move the foot from the accelerator to the brake.

If your vehicle is equipped with a foot rest ("dead pedal") for your left foot, use it. Placing your left foot on the dead pedal will increase the surface area in contact with the vehicle. It will also serve as a brace for spirited driving. If you do not brace yourself with the dead pedal, you must do so with the steering wheel. Using the steering wheel as a support will make smooth steering inputs difficult if not impossible. Pushing on the dead pedal with the left foot will enable you to more accurately apply the appropriate pressure with the right foot on the brake pedal. Finally, pressing on the dead pedal and straightening your knee provides a means for you to raise up off your seat in order to see better as you turn your torso to back the car.

Properly Position Your Hands.

For many years, new drivers were taught to place their hands at the 10:00 o'clock and 2:00 o'clock positions on the steering wheel. This was logical when steering wheels were very large and before power steering minimized the need for leverage when steering.

People trained to drive at 10 and 2 often allow themselves to migrate to 11 and 1, and eventually to one or both hands at 12:00 o'clock. It is impossible to steer smoothly with your hand or hands in this position.

Some instructors insist that the hands should be placed at 8:00 and 4:00 o'clock, arguing that this placement will be the most likely to lessen injury from a deploying air bag. Again, this argument is based on avoiding injury after the collision, rather than avoiding the collision in the first place.

We recommend that you place your hands at 9:00 o'clock and 3:00 o'clock. This provides the greatest control and allows the smoothest inputs because the hands are as far apart as possible. Whenever possible, turn the wheel by simultaneously pushing up with one hand while pulling down with the other.

Since our drivers education days, most of us have probably modified our normal hand position. Many people habitually drive with one hand, often at the

12:00 o'clock position, and the other hand off the wheel altogether. Both hands should be on the wheel whenever possible.

The habit of driving with one hand on the gear shift and one on the wheel should be broken for several reasons. In an emergency you will need the steering wheel first, not the gear shift. Resting your hand on the gear shift knob in a standard transmission vehicle will cause unnecessary wear on the synchronizers. When shifting gears, do not form a fist around the shift knob. Press with the heel of the hand and pull with the fingertips. Do not force the shifter. Once the gears are changed, immediately return your hand to the steering wheel. See the Backing chapter for a description of a recommended method of shifting into reverse.

With your hands at 9 and 3 you can make shallow turns without releasing the grip of either hand. If you were to hold the wheel through a sharp turn, it would force you to cross your arms. You can avoid this by changing the hand positions in anticipation of turns. As you approach a turn, place the hand on the side you are turning toward at the 12:00 o'clock position. Place the other hand at the 6:00 o'clock position. (For a right hand turn, place your right hand at 12:00 o'clock, your left at 6:00 o'clock. For a left hand turn, place your left hand at 12:00 o'clock, your right at 6:00 o'clock.) This will allow you to make a significant turn without the necessity of crossing your arms. When you reach the critical part of the turn your hands will be at approximately 9 and 3. Now you are in the accustomed and comfortable position.

For sharper turns you can "shuffle steer" making sure that you hand the wheel from one hand to the other, ensuring that the right hand is always on the right half of the steering wheel and the left hand is always on the left half. You may find this more difficult than you imagined. Many people have to do this many times slowly before it feels natural and is done smoothly.

Avoid steering with the palm of your hand (with the exception of backing). Grip the steering wheel fairly loosely. You do not have to have a death grip on it to avoid losing control. If you hold it too tightly you will unnecessarily fatigue yourself and negate some of the sensation that you would otherwise feel. It will also be more difficult to impart smooth inputs to the wheel.

Ensure that your thumb and fingertips are in contact with the wheel. These are the most sensitive parts of your hands. Do not wear gloves unless it is extremely cold or you must wear them for some other reason.

Adjust the Mirrors.

Adjust the mirrors prior to moving the car. Mirrors are discussed in more detail later in this chapter.

Most of us are accustomed to providing instructions to the vehicle. If we want to go faster, we press harder on the accelerator. If we want to slow or stop, we press harder on the brake pedal. If we want to turn a sharper corner, we crank more turn into the steering wheel. Many people straighten the front wheels by letting go of the steering wheel. In normal situations all of these techniques will work.

At or beyond the limit of adhesion, however, these approaches will fail you. At the limit of adhesion, applying more throttle will induce an acceleration skid. Applying more brake, when already slowing at the limit of adhesion, will induce a braking skid. When cornering at the limit, turning more will produce a cornering skid. Letting go of the steering wheel to straighten the wheels will result in a sudden jerk as you re-grasp the wheel.

In order to drive well you must accurately interpret information provided by the vehicle. Communications between you and the vehicle are transmitted through all of your senses. More importantly, these same senses are the way you recognize a threat.

BE SENSE ABLE

93

VISION

The most important sense for a driver is sight. Vision is the primary tool for determining not only what is happening within the car but also for determining what is happening outside the car. If I had to choose just one skill that I could improve to make you a better driver, it would be the use of your eyes.

Using your eyes properly allows you to drive smoothly. The importance of driving smoothly when at or near the limit of adhesion cannot be overstated.

Proper use of the eyes involves a visual search pattern

VISUAL SEARCH PATTERN

Far and then near to the front (with the emphasis on far).
The sides.
The instruments, and
The rear (mirrors)

VISION TO THE FRONT

Anyone who has ridden with someone just learning to drive is aware that the new driver is likely to steer erratically. They are constantly correcting and over correcting their input. The reason is simple. Unaccustomed to controlling a vehicle traveling at speed, they tend to focus their attention on the area immediately in front of the vehicle. They pass their point of reference quickly and must find a new one. This results in their constantly adjusting their steering to arrive at constantly changing aiming points. In turn, this results in jerky steering input.

Unaccustomed to regulating speed smoothly, new drivers often accelerate too much and then coast or brake to get back to the desired speed. Often they then slow too much and must accelerate again. This creates a continuously repeating cycle of jarring pedal inputs. Unless corrected, this way of driving becomes a habit that the driver may not be aware of.

Most of us have no concept of how erratically we drive because we unconsciously anticipate the response of the car to our own jerky inputs. The next time you are a passenger take note of the driver's technique. It is probably much jerkier than the driver realizes. It is the reason that one of the best ways to overcome motion sickness in a car is to do the driving yourself. You alleviate the symptoms not because you are such an expert and smooth driver but because you are unconsciously anticipating the otherwise unsettling motions of the car.

Most drivers do not routinely look far enough to the front. The threat is most likely to first appear in front of you. It is usually waiting for you - not following you. The farther ahead you look the sooner you see the threat. The sooner you see the threat, the more time you have to anticipate, prepare, and react. Additionally, the farther ahead you look the smoother your steering will be. You are unlikely to notice anything beyond the point on which you are focusing. If you are staring at the rear of the vehicle to your immediate front, your vision is limited to that distance. If you are looking at the horizon, you will see everything that takes place between you and the horizon.

In addition to the things that you might normally look for while you are driving, add alternative routes. An alternative route may be a detour. It could also be the shoulder of the road, the sidewalk, the median, a vacant lot, or any of the other places a vehicle can be driven. In an emergency, the road is just a convenience.

VISION TO THE SIDES

Many people drive as if their necks were paralyzed. The side windows are there for a reason. Use them. Later we will discuss looking around a corner as you approach it.

VISION TO THE REAR

Mirrors are critical in detecting threats. Your goal should be to always know what is around your vehicle. This means that you must check your mirrors every few seconds. Assuming that your vehicle is equipped with the normal complement of three mirrors, you need only apply an inexpensive stick-on convex ("fish eye") mirror to eliminate all blind spots. Attach the stick-on mirror to the flat driver's side mirror.

Now, seated in the normal driving position, you should be able to keep a person in view as he walks completely around the vehicle. As he crosses in front of the vehicle he is in your frontal vision. Going to the front passenger's side of the car he is in your peripheral vision until he appears in the convex passenger's side mirror. By the time his image leaves this mirror, it appears in the interior rearview mirror. As the image leaves the interior mirror, it is picked up in the driver's flat side mirror. It then appears in the aftermarket stick-on convex mirror. Finally, the person appears in the driver's peripheral vision.

Some people adjust their side mirrors so that the trailing edges of their vehicle's rear quarter panels are just visible on the inside edge of the mirror. Advocates of this approach argue that the edge of the quarter panel provides a reference point. With this as a reference, the driver always knows exactly where the item in the mirror actually is in relation to his own vehicle. With this technique there is generally an overlap between the areas covered by the side mirrors and that covered by the rearview mirror.

Others argue that this creates an unnecessary duplication between the interior edges of the side mirrors and the exterior edges of the interior rearview mirror. They also argue that this creates blind spots to the sides. These people prefer to adjust the side mirrors farther out. This is done by the driver leaning toward, and resting his head on, his side window. He then adjusts the driver's side mirror so that he can just see the rear edge of the rear quarter panel on that side. He then leans away from that window approximately the same distance as he leaned toward the window. He then adjusts the passenger's side mirror in the same manner. Those who advocate this system argue that it eliminates both the blind spots and the overlapping of fields of view.

Either approach is workable but before deciding on the mirrors angled farther out approach, consider the advantage of keeping an eye on your vulnerable quarter panel. Perhaps having more than one mirror showing the area of the rear quarter panels is not such a bad idea.

Look where you want to go.

A critical rule for proper use of the eyes is to look where you want to go. Often in single car accidents, the car strikes the only hazard off the edge of the road. The driver's natural tendency is to focus on the hazard. The driver has also unconsciously trained himself to steer toward wherever he is looking. In this case it is the very object that he hopes to avoid.

In drivers education you were probably taught that, in a skid, you should "turn in the direction of the skid." Technically, this advice is correct. However, the instructor probably failed to mention how far to turn. Not far enough and you continue skidding as before. Too far and you induce a secondary skid in the opposite direction. Usually this secondary skid is worse than the original skid was. Better advice than "turn in the direction of the skid" would be "look where you want to go." The tendency mentioned above to steer toward where you are looking will help ensure the appropriate steering for skid recovery.

INSTRUMENTS

In addition to looking to the front, sides, and rear, the driver must include an occasional glance at the instrument panel as part of the visual search pattern. Researchers conducted a study to determine the effects of fog on a driver's ability to estimate speed. Test subjects were provided a screen and an accelerator. With the accelerator they could adjust the speed at which the scenery on the screen approached. The test subjects could not see a speedometer. They were told to adjust the speed to approximate a car traveling at 70 miles an hour. The test subjects were extremely accurate with their estimates. On average they were within a few miles an hour of the target speed. The researchers then introduced fog in the scenery and again asked the drivers to make the scenery approach at 70 miles an hour. Most of us would expect that people would naturally tend to drive slower in the foggy conditions. In fact, the drivers averaged 90 miles an hour. According to the report, in reduced visibility two portions of the brain play tricks on each other, defeating the normal ability to estimate speed.

It is good to be looking, but what are you looking for in addition to normal traffic hazards? That question is answered in the chapter on COMMENTARY DRIVING.

FEEL

After vision, the most important sense to the driver is the sense of feel. Unfortunately most drivers ignore what they feel and automobile manufacturers try to design at least "road feel" out of the vehicle in an effort to make the ride comfortable.

The primary, though not the only, reason to pay attention to what you are feeling is to recognize the weight transfer of the vehicle. This is discussed at greater length later. Feeling how smoothly or abruptly the weight shifts will be an important factor in our ability to drive more smoothly.

HEARING

Hearing, important for everyday driving, is critical in a high threat environment. You need to hear what is going on around you. Again, the vehicle manufacturer has exacerbated your problem. In this case, sound deadening materials have been added to isolate you from the sound outside the vehicle.

Do not compound the problem. In critical parts of your route - places where you have predicted you are most vulnerable to attack - make sure that you turn off the vehicle's sound system and turn off any fans or other noise producing devices. Close your windows. While this may sound contradictory, you will hear more through a closed window than you will hear as the wind whistles though an open window. There are other reasons to ensure the windows are closed which are covered later.

SMELL

The sense of smell is used less often but you will employ it as you inspect the vehicle prior to driving and as an indicator of mechanical or electrical problems as you drive. If in your initial inspection you detect a strange odor or a smell like fireworks, get away from the vehicle. While driving the acrid odor of melting insulation, smoldering belts, or fuel or anti-freeze vapors are all indications of problems that need to be addressed.

DRIVING HABITS

The techniques described in the DRIVING BASICS chapter must become habit.

MODIFICATIONS

Ideally, a vehicle driven in a dangerous area should undergo extensive modification. Usually such changes are impractical and unlikely to be made. The list of possibilities is almost endless. We recommend two primary modifications. They are the small convex stick-on mirrors previously addressed and appropriate tire pressure.

TIRE PRESSURE

According to the National Highway Transportation Safety Administration (NHTSA), "27 percent of passenger cars on U.S. roadways are driven with one or more substantially under-inflated tires. In addition...33 percent of light trucks (including sport utility vehicles, vans and pickup trucks) are driven with one or more substantially under-inflated tires." A 2007 tire industry survey indicated that 85 percent of drivers fail to "properly" check tire pressure. A visual inspection of tires is not sufficient to determine if the tire is properly inflated. The development of the tire pressure monitoring system (TPMS) has mitigated, but not eliminated, this problem.

Since tires often loose air, developing the habit of frequently checking your vehicle's tire pressure is very important. Remember everything the vehicle is primarily designed to do (go, stop, and turn) is done at the tire contact patch. The tire pressure recommended by your vehicle's maker can be found on the door edge or sill and in the driver's manual. These are "cold" pressures. This means that the tires have not been driven more than one mile in the preceding three hours. As the tires are driven at speed they heat up, increasing the tire pressure. It is the pressure at normal driving temperature that is considered important. The "cold" recommendations are those that will result in a proper warm tire pressure after some period of driving at speed.

The proper pressure is that listed in the vehicle's placard or manual. However, if the most critical driving will probably be done when the tires are still cold, the cold tires should be inflated to whatever pressure they would have at their normal running temperature. Remembering that the vast majority of attacks take place in the morning, near the residence, on the way to work, it is obvious that an attack is most likely to take place at the time when the tires are the coldest. Therefore, we can consider inflating the tires closer to the ideal warm pressure when the tires are cold. Another reason to increase the tire pressure over the vehicle manufacturer's recommendations is that air pressure is likely to decrease over time as it slowly leaks out of the tire. (Air never leaks into a tire.) If anything (disregarding changes in the ambient air temperature), the tire pressure will be less than it was the last time you checked. Therefore, for our purposes, the best pressure is probably *slightly* (no more than three psi) above the vehicle manufacturer's recommendation.

There are a number of problems with under inflated tires. They include an increased risk of catastrophic tire failure, an increased chance of rolling the tire off its rim which could result in rolling the vehicle, and hydroplaning at a slower speed. Pumping the tires up slightly beyond the recommended pressure but not beyond their maximum pressure will result in a slightly harsher ride. Increasing the air pressure dramatically could also result in decreased traction since the tire will tend to bulge in the center of the tread. More information is at https://www.nhtsa.gov/equipment/tires.

AVOIDING STOPS

It is preferable to avoid stopping whenever possible. It takes more time to get away from a dead stop than from a slow roll. Some students have told me, "When I'm overseas, I never stop for anything." I am sure that these students will never become the victims of a terrorist attack. They will become the victims of a traffic accident long before the terrorists can get to them. Clearly, in most cases, you should stop at stop signs, stop lights, etc. However, if you can time the light so that you do not actually have to come to a full stop you will be better prepared to leave quickly if you must. Again, you will not have done it when you need it most unless you have made it a habit.

WHEN STOPPED

Whenever you must stop, be sure to leave enough room to the front of your vehicle so that you can maneuver around the vehicle in front without having to back up. As a general rule, stop far enough back so that you can see where the rear tires of the vehicle to your front touch the road. This will not only allow maneuver room, it will be the nearly perfect distance from which to initiate a ram of that vehicle, should that become necessary.

Leave your vehicle in gear whenever stopping momentarily. Shifting an automatic transmission into park means that you will have to depress the brake pedal and manipulate the gear shift lever to get it back into drive. Having a standard transmission vehicle in neutral and taking your foot off the clutch pedal means that you will have to depress the clutch and shift it into gear before you can move. This time is critical in an emergency. As you slow for a stop in a vehicle with a manual transmission, you should progressively downshift to the gear appropriate for immediate acceleration.

WINDOWS UP, DOORS LOCKED

More than one life has been saved by the mere fact that the intended victims had their windows up and doors locked. Rather than leave a crack open at the top of the windows it is preferable for them to be completely rolled up. This will increase the effective strength of the windows. With the window opened even as little as an inch, the whistling wind will interfere with your ability to hear what is happening outside the car.

The doors should be locked for obvious reasons. If your vehicle has self-locking doors, remember that not every car you ever drive will be similarly equipped. Get in the habit of physically locking and then checking your doors rather than relying on the self-locking mechanism.

PARK TACTICALLY

You should be in the habit of carefully studying the surrounding area whenever you park. As long as you remain in your vehicle you can use it to evade or counter a threat.   Since you are able to at least superficially examine the area around your parking space, you can take your time.   If a problem develops, you will be able to move quickly. For these reasons it is generally preferable to back into parking spaces ("tactical" parking). This allows you to leave quickly by driving forward out of the space. It is not always possible or practical to park tactically but develop the habit of parking that way whenever possible.

SOUND SYSTEM, AIR CONDITIONER, AND FANS OFF

In critical parts of the route (See the ROUTE ANALYSIS chapter), turn off the sound system, air conditioner, and fans. As mentioned earlier, your ability to hear and concentrate on what is going on around you will be enhanced by eliminating unnecessary noise. Air conditioning will not only hamper your ability to hear, it will also drain power that might be needed to evade or counter. Even unconsciously we may be distracted by sound. Studies show that drivers Looking for an address or street sign will often intuitively turn their car radio down or off to help them concentrate.

PROPER USE OF EYES

A common bad habit is the improper use of our eyes as we drive. The principles which you should make habits are discussed in the chapters on DRIVING BASICS and COMMENTARY DRIVING. They include:

Look well to the front.
Drive smoothly.
Check the mirrors frequently.
Know what surrounds you.
Look where you want to go.
Do not look at what you want to avoid.

FUEL

Keep the tank at least one-half and preferably three-quarters full.

VEHICLE DYNAMICS

TIRES AND TRACTION

In many respects, the most important part of any vehicle is the tires. If a vehicle is chiefly designed to go, stop, and turn, then it can be said that everything the car is primarily intended to do is done by the tires. It is the tire contact patches – the area of rubber in contact with the road – where all of these are controlled.

In a resting, evenly balanced car, with matching tires, the tire contact patches will be about the same size.

If you accelerate a vehicle forward from a stop, the center of gravity of the vehicle will shift (the preponderance of weight will transfer) toward the rear of the vehicle. This will place greater weight on the rear tires. Because the tires are pneumatic, adding weight will enlarge the size of the tire contact patch. The effect is similar to holding a balloon between the palms of your hands. As you press your hands together, the area of the balloon in contact with your hands increases. Since traction is largely a function of the amount of rubber in contact with the road, accelerating will increase the traction of the rear tires. At the same time, because the weight is shifting away from the front of the vehicle, the size of the front tire contact patch decreases. The traction available to the front tires is decreased.

When a car is going forward and is slowed, the center of gravity will move forward. The size (and therefore, traction) of the front tire contact patches is increased. The size (and therefore, traction) of the rear tires is decreased.

Finally, when a car turns, the center of gravity will shift to the outside of the turn. Therefore, the outside tires will have greater traction than will the inside tires.

It is a slight over simplification to equate "going" with "accelerating," "stopping" with "braking," and "turning" with "cornering."   However, using these words (accelerating, braking, and cornering) allows us to refer to the "ABCs of traction management."

THE ABC'S OF TRACTION MANAGEMENT
Accelerating
Braking
Cornering

A final, and very important, factor affecting traction is the smoothness with which accelerating, braking, and cornering inputs are applied. Anyone who has spent some time on an iced-over parking lot as a teenager knows that you can induce a skid by simply jerking the steering wheel an inch or jabbing the accelerator or brake.

There is a finite amount of traction available to you at any given time. Use of 100 percent of that traction results in driving at the "limit of adhesion." Exceeding the limit of adhesion results in a skid.

If you accelerate too rapidly, especially in a front-wheel driven vehicle, you are likely to induce an acceleration skid.   The front tires, which have reduced traction because the weight is shifted to the rear during acceleration, may exceed the limit of adhesion and spin uselessly until they finally grip and the vehicle begins to move.

In a vehicle without an anti-lock braking system (ABS), if you brake too hard you are likely to induce a braking skid. The wheels lock, the tires stop rotating and slide on the road surface. The resulting friction quickly melts the rubber and the tire slides on the molten rubber. This is a very inefficient way to stop the vehicle.

If you corner too hard, centrifugal force will cause the vehicle to slide toward the outside of the turn. The critical tires in avoiding this drift are those that are supplying the effective traction – the outside tires. Therefore, it is critical that, at least when driving at the limit of adhesion, you place the outside tires on that area of the road surface which provides sufficient traction. If you must drive over a patch of ice, given a choice, put the inside tires on the ice. Although drifting sideways as you corner gives the impression that you are traveling as quickly as possible, in fact the sideward skid is actually scrubbing off speed that would be more efficiently used to go forward.

You can combine a couple of these factors. You can accelerate or brake while cornering. However, if you use X percent of the available traction for cornering, you cannot use more than the remaining traction (100% - X%) for braking or accelerating without inducing a skid.

Generally, the fastest you can drive is at the limit of adhesion. If you attempt to drive faster you will actually go slower because you have lost traction.

Since we routinely drive nowhere near the point where a skid would be induced, most of us are poorly prepared for driving at or near the limit. For example, you have probably unconsciously conditioned yourself to believe that if you want to stop the car you push on the brake pedal. If you want to stop sooner, you push harder. In a non-ABS equipped vehicle, if you are already at or beyond the limit of adhesion, pushing the brake harder will be less effective than releasing some of the pressure on the brake pedal.

If you find yourself trying to brake and corner beyond the limit of adhesion, your natural reaction is to push harder on the brake and turn the steering wheel even more. In fact, if all four wheels are skidding, pushing the brake harder and turning the wheel farther will only serve to give you something to do as your car continues to slide in whatever direction it happened to be traveling when the wheels began to skid.

When driving near or beyond the limit of adhesion, which tire or tires have the greatest or least traction is a critical issue. If, for example, you brake hard and corner at the same time the tire with the greatest traction will be the front outside tire. That with the least will be the inside rear tire. If one tire and one tire only begins to skid, all other considerations being equal, it is most likely to be the one with the least traction, in this case the inside rear. If only that tire skids it will not result in a control problem. That tire was providing very little of the overall traction.

If both front tires lose traction it results in an under steer skid, sometimes referred to as "pushing" or "plowing". The vehicle may be described as "tight." The front wheels may be turned but the vehicle will tend to continue traveling the direction it was traveling when traction was lost. The easiest way to remember this is to think of the vehicle as under responding to your steering input or "under steering."

If both rear tires lose traction it results in an over steer skid. If there is any turn at all in the front wheels the rear of the vehicle slides and the "rear end comes around." The easiest way to remember this is to think of the vehicle as over responding to your steering input or "over steering." A vehicle which tends to over steer may be referred to as "loose."

COMMENTARY DRIVING

Commentary driving calls for talking to yourself while you drive. Its primary purpose is to keep you conscious of immediate threats or, as one true expert put it, "To keep you alive right now!" It also has several additional advantages. It is a good way to familiarize you with an area. It is also a good way to maintain basic traffic safety because it ensures that you are always aware of what is going on around you. (The technique was originally developed primarily for this purpose.)

Studies have shown that, when you are exposed to a stimulus through more than one of your senses it makes a greater impact and you remember it longer. In order for this technique to work you must actually speak aloud so that you hear yourself describing what you see. Seeing something and thinking about it or mouthing a description under your breath is not nearly as effective as seeing something and hearing yourself say something about it.

Combining commentary driving with the skills addressed in the OBSERVATION SKILLS chapter is an effective way of remaining alert to the indicators of danger around you. It is the surest way to place yourself in condition yellow (relaxed but alert).

What should you comment on? In all cases your primary objective is immediate or developing potential threats. There is almost always something to comment on since any number of situations could develop into a threat. For example, if you cannot see around the next bend, or over the next crest, or there is a hidden drive, all could develop into a simple traffic safety problem, if not a terrorist or criminal assault. Looking for these situations will help you avoid routine driving problems as well as more sinister threats.

You should not only comment on what you are seeing, but on what you are doing. If, for example, you are moving to the inside edge of your lane to see farther around the upcoming corner, you should say that you are doing this. If you are checking your mirror, you should say, "mirror." You should be talking constantly.

> **Limit point** - The farthest point to which you have an unobstructed view of the road.

Even though the limit point is as far as you can see the road, often there are indicators beyond the limit point that suggest where the road may go beyond where it is in view. For example, you may see the upper portion of vehicles beyond the limit point. Power lines, lampposts, or tree lines that parallel the road and that are visible beyond the limit point may indicate lower elevation, or a right or left hand turn.

Your eyes should be scanning:

1. Beyond the limit point, then

2. To the limit point, then

3. To the area between your vehicle and the limit point, then

4. To your immediate front and sides, then

5. To your controls and, finally

6. To the mirrors before repeating the cycle.

As you repeat this process, objects that were far away are nearer and may deserve another comment. They may also deserve a comment as you pass and again as you see them in your mirror. You could mention the same object several times. However, avoid the tendency to spend too much time on any one object. It may well be a distraction from something more threatening.

If your vehicle is equipped with a global positioning system (GPS) device, you may find it extremely helpful. Often as you approach a blind curve or crest it is not possible to determine what direction the road takes beyond the limit point. A properly positioned GPS screen allows you to take a quick glance to determine where the road goes beyond the limit point. It may also show intersections which would otherwise not be seen until later. Make sure you only take a quick glance. It is easy to become mesmerized by the GPS and lose track of the real world around you. Also do not rely on the GPS to show you everything you need to know. It should only be used as an indicator of some things that may lie ahead.

As you practice this technique you will find yourself developing short descriptions. A typical commentary driving session could include something like the following:

> "Limit point - Crest. Hidden drive right. Fog lines. Mirror - One car my lane.

> "Limit point - Constant curve to left. Drive[way] right. Drive cleared. Intersection – Appears clear. Parked car, left. Oncoming car. No passing zone in both directions. Reduced speed ahead. Hidden drive left. Mirror - same car now closing.

> "Limit point - Crest. Woods to edge of road right. Maneuver room off-road, left. Woods on right. Mirrors - Following car turned off.

> "Limit point - Crest. Road appears to curve right beyond the limit point. Bend to right - Closing on limit point. Pedestrian right – hands empty. Mirror - Motorcycle closing.

"Limit point - Blind crest. GPS - Road bends right beyond crest and intersects another road. Van right - Could block road. Mirrors - Clear."

As you are conducting your initial area familiarization you should be constantly commenting. You should be looking for patterns of activity to include; traffic patterns, pedestrian activity, street vendors, etc. On later travel along this same route you will be looking for changes in these patterns. Look for alternate routes, safe havens, danger areas, areas conducive to surveillance activities, and potential attack sites. Vary the times of surveys to determine changes based on the hour. Keep in mind that you must avoid establishing patterns of activity.

For some, commentary driving is difficult at first. Perhaps they feel self conscious. Others seem to infer that because the technique is extremely simple, it cannot be all that effective. In order for commentary driving to be useful, you must practice it. Do not allow it to become an exercise in just mentioning obvious threats. Look for indicators that a threat may be developing.

```
┌─────────────────────────────────────────────┐
│                                               │
│      ROUTE ANALYSIS COMMENTARY DRIVING        │
│                                               │
│  Look for and describe out loud:              │
│          Potential and actual threats.        │
│          Traffic patterns.                    │
│          Pedestrian activity.                 │
│          Other activities (street vendors,    │
│          crowds, children playing, people     │
│          loitering, etc.).                    │
│          Alternate routes (to include         │
│          drivable unpaved terrain - shoulders,│
│          median, etc.).                       │
│          Safe havens.                         │
│          Danger areas.                        │
│          Potential surveillance sites.        │
│          Potential attack sites.              │
│                                               │
└─────────────────────────────────────────────┘
```

You will find that using this technique is surprisingly tiring. It is not because of physical exertion. After all, you are just driving a car and talking to yourself. You are, however, also forcing yourself to concentrate more than would be your normal practice. Contrasting your weariness after commentary driving with your normal fatigue from driving without commentary dramatically shows this increase in concentration. Because it is so tiring, you will probably not want to employ commentary driving all the time. At a minimum you should use it whenever you are in a particularly dangerous area – whenever you are traversing a critical part of your route. With frequent practice you will find that it improves your observation skills significantly, even when you are not actually commenting.

If there is more than one person in the vehicle, it is usually preferable for passengers to limit their commentary to developing and imminent threats. The driver's comments would include everything discussed above. Each person should be assigned a sector of responsibility. These sectors should overlap to ensure complete coverage. A passenger in the front seat is responsible for the front quadrant on his or her side. Passengers in the rear are responsible for their respective sides and rear of the vehicle. It is critical that each person maintain vigilance of their respective sector. Remember, when the distraction is from one direction, the threat may be from another.

As the driver, it is critical that you talk continuously while employing this technique. This forces you to continue scanning and ensures you do not fixate on a distraction.

HIGH PERFORMANCE DRIVING

When all of your attempts to avoid trouble have failed, the next best option is to evade. In a vehicle, this may mean driving fast to get away from a threat. Simply driving fast, however, is not an adequate solution. Most car chases end in either the person being chased surrendering (as in the case of an arrest), the pursuer giving up the chase, or one or both of the participants crashing.

If the only reason to study and practice high performance driving were the possibility that you might someday be chased, we could treat the subject similarly to firearms and martial arts – a nice thing to know but not something that will probably be needed. Being chased a significant distance by an attacker is a fairly remote possibility. Usually, moving out of the immediate area planned for the assault (the "X") is sufficient to disrupt their plans and foil the attack.

We strongly recommend using high performance driving for another reason as well. Once you have developed the techniques to the point where you are relatively comfortable with them, you will realize that you cannot practice these techniques without constantly being aware of what is far out to your front. You must see and analyze at least as far as the next turn - or where you think the next turn may be if it is hidden from view. This means that you will be looking far to the front and as far as possible beyond the turns. Using these techniques, you can outrun an attacker. More importantly, you can detect a threat much earlier. The early detection may allow you to avoid the threat. Being aware of your surroundings may be all that is necessary to save your life. It is difficult to remain alert if you are on "autopilot." When practicing the skills we will discuss, it is impossible not to be alert.

For our purposes, "high performance driving" will be defined as driving using techniques which will allow you to drive a car fast. It may seem like quibbling but the distinction between driving fast and driving using high performance techniques is significant. We suggest that you always drive using high performance driving techniques but that you only drive fast when necessary to avoid a threat or when in an environment designed specifically for driving fast (i.e., the race track).

Many people believe that driving fast, even before recognizing a threat, will somehow protect them. While loitering or driving excessively slowly offers no advantage, driving exceedingly fast makes you more vulnerable – not less. There are several reasons for this:

Excessive speed:

Reduces the visual advantage.
Speed limits peripheral vision as well as the ability to process what is seen peripherally. Some have suggested that, if when stationary you have almost 180 degrees of effective peripheral vision, at 80 miles per hour you have only 30 degrees.

Reduces reaction time and space.
Speed limits your reaction time and space when a threat ahead is finally identified.

Limits the available options.

Increases the chance of an accident.
Speed significantly increases the probability of being in a non-attack related accident. Often, even in environments where terrorism and other crimes are rampant, traffic accidents pose an even greater threat.

High performance techniques – those techniques which are used to drive as quickly as possible – can be used every time you drive a vehicle. You do not have to drive fast to practice most of the techniques which allow you to drive fast. In fact, you can conform to all of the traffic laws and do it so that no one is even aware that you are using the techniques. If you do not practice the techniques to the point that they have become habit, you will not employ them when you need them.

> **Safe haven** - A place where a potential victim of an attack may go but where attackers would probably not go.

Before running, make sure you have somewhere to run to. Safe havens are places where you can go but where an assailant is unlikely to go. What type of place will make a good safe haven depends on the local environment. They *may* include:

Police stations, assuming a friendly relationship with the local police and assuming those chasing you would be reluctant to attack the police.

Fire stations.

Hospitals, particularly emergency rooms of hospitals.

Crowded areas. (But only if the attackers intend to attack only specific individuals. If the attackers are content to cause indiscriminate damage, crowded areas should be avoided.)

Your embassy or that of a friendly nation.

High security areas such as military or other government installations. (Be aware that the approach to guarded facilities must be done very carefully. You could appear to be the threat rather than the victim.)

TRACTION MANAGEMENT

A primary principle to remember is that a vehicle can go the fastest when it is going in the straightest possible line. If the wheels are straight, all available traction can be used for acceleration. If the front wheels are turned, some of the available traction is necessarily being devoted to cornering.

You can only approach the full performance potential of a vehicle by skillfully managing the available traction between the tire contact patches and the road surface. A complete understanding of the points presented in the chapter on VEHICLE DYNAMICS is essential to an understanding of high performance driving techniques.

THE LINE

Most of us routinely drive down the center of our lane and think nothing of it. If you are to drive as fast as possible (to evade an attacker) there is a better "line" to drive. By properly positioning your vehicle in the roadway you can significantly increase your speed.

There is no secret to going fast in a straight line. Simply – (1) Keep the front tires pointed as straight as possible and (2) Push the accelerator to the floor. We all realize, however, that keeping the pedal to the floor as we negotiate a turn will result in problems. Races, including races to evade an attacker, are won or lost in the corners. Proper cornering is based on the principle that a car goes the fastest when it goes the straightest. As a corollary, the less time spent with the front wheels turned, the faster you will get to your destination.

GEOMETRIC OR CONSTANT RADIUS TURN

Geometric line – A driving line in which the turn begins at the outer edge of the available road space (entry) and, using a constant amount of turn, clips the inside edge (geometric apex), and the outside edge (exit), without changing the initial turn of the wheel. It is used to maintain the speed developed in the long straight leading into the corner.

The fastest way to negotiate a corner is to start with the outside tires on the outside edge of the available road space, turn the steering wheel so that the inside tires will clip the inside edge of the available road surface and then the outside wheels will just touch the outside edge of the available road surface.

The "geometric" turn is a "constant radius" turn. Once the turn is cranked into the steering wheel, the wheel remains turned the same amount until it is straightened at the completion of the turn. Although this is clearly not a straight line, it is the straightest line possible from the entry to the exit of the turn. The straightest line is the fastest line through the corner. Assuming the driver is at the limit of adhesion (going as fast as possible without losing traction), he cannot start to accelerate until he is turning less. He will hold a constant amount of turn until beginning to straighten the wheel on reaching the exit of the corner. Then, and only then, as he straightens the wheel and uses less cornering traction, will he have traction available to accelerate.

The geometric turn (or an even earlier apex than the geometric apex) is useful when trying to maintain the advantage of a long straight leading into the turn. It allows the speed from the straight to be maintained longer (fast in – slow out).

LATE APEX OR INCREASING RADIUS TURN

Late apex or increasing radius turn - A driving line in which the entry, apex, and exit are all later than would be the case in a geometric turn. It is used to allow earlier acceleration onto a long straight following the corner.

An alternative way to negotiate the turn would be to enter later, apex later, and exit later. This turn begins as a relatively sharp turn but, before the apex is reached, it is possible to start unwinding (straightening) the steering wheel. As the turn progresses the radius gets longer (an increasing radius turn). Clearly one would have to enter this turn slower than the geometric turn. However, since the radius is increasing at that point where the driver can start to unwind the steering wheel, he can accelerate sooner. As soon as he starts to straighten the wheel, more traction is available for acceleration. The advantage gained by using an increasing radius and accelerating earlier will carry through the entire following straightaway to the next turn. This is often referred to as the "late apex" or "increasing radius" line. It is particularly useful when a turn is particularly sharp and when a turn is followed by a long straightaway. This turn allows earlier acceleration onto the longer straightaway (slow in – fast out).

The late apex or increasing radius line is more difficult for most drivers than it would appear. Most people habitually enter corners early and turn the wheel through the entire corner. It is fairly easy to determine when you have entered such a turn too early. If it is necessary to hold the turn in the steering wheel to the apex or beyond, you entered too early. You should be unwinding the steering wheel, aiming for the exit, and accelerating prior to reaching the apex. Do not hold the turn in the steering wheel longer than necessary. Remember, the car goes the fastest when it goes the straightest. If you enter a corner too late it becomes apparent when there is no need to drive to the exit (when you end the turn on the inside of the available road space rather than the outside).

STRAIGHTENING THE ROAD

Some turns can be ignored by driving the straightest line possible (straightening the turn). In some cases the roadway may be so winding that attempting to enter on the outside edge of the available road space, apex on the inside edge, and exit on the outside edge will result in even more turning of the steering wheel than would result from simply driving from apex to apex to apex.

COMPROMISING A TURN

When one turn is followed immediately by another, it may be impossible to drive a perfect line through both turns. In this case, one of the turns is compromised in order to maximize the benefits of the other. That turn which must be driven as precisely as possible is the one that is preceded or followed by the longer straightaway. For example, in the case of a longer straight following the second turn, the turn at the end of the shorter (first) straight is compromised to maximize the line through the second turn – the one leading onto the longer straight. (Slow in – fast out.)

UNDERSTANDING COMMON CORNERING ERRORS

Driving the line properly is a trial and error process. If you recognize your mistakes each time you turn a specific corner, you can improve the next time you negotiate the same corner.

ENTERING TOO EARLY

As stated above, the most common error that we see is the tendency to enter the corner too early. If, in a late apex turn, you find that you are still turning the wheel, or holding the turn you have already applied, at the apex, you have entered too early.

ALLOWING THE OUTSIDE EDGE OF THE ROAD TO DICTATE THE TURN

Too early an entry is sometimes caused by the driver entering the turn because the outside edge of the road begins to turn at that point. This will usually result in entering the turn too early. Look through the apex to the exit to determine where to enter.

ENTERING FROM THE MIDDLE OF THE ROAD

Allowing yourself to stray from the outer edge to the center of the available road space as you approach the turn is a common problem. Its effect is similar to that of entering the corner too early – you must steer as or after you pass the apex. The outside tires should be on the outside edge of the available road space until committed to the turn.

ENTERING TOO LATE

If, after making the turn, you find yourself pointed down the straightaway but on the inside of the available road space, you have either entered too late or have held the turn longer than necessary.

JERKY INPUTS TO THE STEERING WHEEL

If you find yourself sawing on the steering wheel (rather than applying a smooth consistent input and unwinding just as smoothly) you are probably not looking beyond the corner. If your head and eyes remain fixed in the direction the car is traveling, you necessarily focus on a series of aiming points as you turn. This forces you to steer incrementally rather than smoothly.

TOO MUCH OR TOO LITTLE STEERING

If you find that you are turning at the proper entry but either go so deep that you must unwind the steering wheel to avoid going off the road to the inside, or you go wide of the apex, you are not looking through the apex to the exit. You are probably concentrating more on when you want to turn than you are on looking where you want to go.

STREET LINE DRIVING

One on-line site makes the following argument against using the "racing line" on public roads:

"The 'racing line' that is used on racetracks is the fastest route through a curve, using the full physical width of the road. Is this a good idea for getting around curves on public roads? No, it is ludicrous, yet we have found it suggested online, by professional people who merely *think* they know about in-depth road safety." (http://www.driveandstayalive.com/info%20section/news/x 050712 racing-drivers-are-not-road-safety-experts op-ed ew.htm)

Obviously this is a valid point *if* we define the available road surface as "the full physical width of the road" (as would normally be the case on a racetrack). If, however, we define the available road space as your lane, and if that lane is wider than your vehicle, you can safely practice driving the line every time you drive. You would not ever use your whole lane if oncoming traffic were on the edge of their lane where you have picked for your entry, apex, or exit.

We are creatures of habit. We do not suddenly break habits in an emergency. If you continue to drive down the center of your lane you will not use the faster line in an emergency.

BLIND TURNS

If you are actually being pursued by a would-be attacker, you may choose to use more of the road than would otherwise be legal. You must be very careful about crossing into the oncoming lane. Where you drive on the right and the driver's seat is on the left of the vehicle, as in the US, you may be able to cheat a little on blind right hand turns. Because you are on the left side of our vehicle and in the left lane we can see farther around a right hand turn. As long as you are not at the limit of adhesion you may be able to slip back into your lane before colliding with the oncoming traffic.

In a blind left hand turn you cannot turn in to the oncoming lane as early as you might like. You may not be able to return to your lane in time to avoid the head-on collision.

OTHER CONSIDERATIONS

You cannot simply drive as fast as the car can go, even if you use a good line. You intuitively know that you cannot enter a 90 degree corner at over 100 miles per hour. You need to slow the car so that you can enter the corner at a manageable speed. You want that speed to be as fast as you can take the corner on the proper line and go as fast as possible as long as possible before applying the brake. The majority of the braking must be done on the straightaway prior to turning into the corner. Ideally, you will smoothly (but quickly) squeeze down on the brake until reaching that point just short of locking the wheels (or engaging the ABS) is being applied. You will then brake until you are ready to turn at the appropriate entry with the appropriate speed.

Some drivers will immediately begin to accelerate as they begin the turn. This will work at normal driving speeds and overcomes the potential problems of braking and turning at the same time. In a late apex turn, however, there is a very real danger of inducing an under steer skid by accelerating immediately. The acceleration transfers weight to the rear tires and off of the front tires. Traction is increased in the rear and reduced in the front of the car. At the very moment that you are trying to get the front tires to grip to turn the car, you are reducing the traction of the front tires. This can be avoided by trail braking. Trail braking is a technique in which the driver continues to brake (actually trails off on the brake pressure) while adding steering. The braking should be concluded at the point in the turn where the driver starts to unwind the steering wheel. At this point, because the traction being used for steering is reduced, additional traction is available for acceleration.

In a geometric (constant radius) turn the steering input remains constant. This allows you to accelerate or decelerate as required to stay at the limit of adhesion. Trail braking, therefore, is not necessary in a properly performed geometric turn.

Trail braking must be done carefully to avoid the combination of steering and braking exceeding the limit of adhesion. If, for example, 90 percent of the available traction is used for steering, no more than 10 percent can be used for trail braking. Experience with students has shown that this is a relatively difficult skill to master. At slow speeds the student knows intuitively that it is not necessary to trail brake. Not braking becomes habit and it is difficult to continue braking in a turn even when needed. This skill must be mastered at slow speeds in order to be properly applied at greater speeds.

In addition to hard braking, other tasks should be accomplished on the straight. The less you have to do as you negotiate the corner, the better. These tasks include downshifting (in a standard transmission vehicle), pre-positioning your hands (covered in the chapter on DRIVING BASICS), and turning your head and eyes to look as far beyond the corner as possible. As you brake on the straight prior to the turn you can downshift to the gear that will be required when you accelerate (at that point just short of the apex where you will begin to unwind the steering).

PRACTICE

Mastering proper driving techniques, like becoming a skilled martial artist or marksman, requires practice. Most of us are unable to devote the time needed to become expert in fighting skills. However, most of us drive almost every day. According to the American Automobile Association (AAA), Americans spend an average of over 48 minutes per day driving. (Johnson, 2016.) If that time is spent building and reinforcing good habits its easy to see how we can significantly improve our driving ability. As stated previously, guns and hand-to-hand fighting are only effective in countering an attack. Driving can be used to avoid or evade an attack. It can also be used to counter many attacks. We may or may not be able to disable an assailant with a 9mm bullet or a roundhouse kick. It is significantly easier to counter an attacker with a two-ton vehicle.

BACKING

When driving and on the "X" (in the "kill zone") of an ambush, you have three options available. You can stop on the X - the worst possible choice. You are exactly where the assailant wants you to be. You *must* move. You can move forward, unless you are somehow constrained from doing so. You can back up. Since backing may be the only viable option, it is critical that you are able to back quickly and precisely.

UNDERSTANDING THE PROBLEMS OF BACKING

For many, backing is the most difficult task in driving. There are several reasons for the problems encountered when we attempt to make a car go backwards. Vehicles are designed primarily to move forward. With less emphasis on parallel parking in the drivers' education of teenage Americans, most drivers are even less adept at backing than in the past. Some problems in backing are related to our inability to adequately see where we are going. This has worsened with the new design of vehicles in which the rear of the vehicle is much higher than in years past. It is aggravated by the awkward position that one must assume to look to the rear while seated in a vehicle. It is also the result of the confusion caused by the steering required. We have encountered more and more students who do not

141

have the slightest idea which way to turn the wheel as they back around a curve. This is exacerbated by those who attempt to alternate looking over one shoulder, then the other, then at one or more of their mirrors.

In addition to the factors mentioned above, there are several other factors which mitigate against easily driving a car in REVERSE, they include, front end swing out, caster, and weight transfer.

FRONT END SWING OUT

When driving forward we steer the leading end of the vehicle. When backing, we steer the trailing end of the vehicle. Because of this geometry, it would be more difficult to back a vehicle than drive it forward even without the other factors that must be considered. In order to discuss front end swing out it is instructive to first examine what happens as a car negotiates a curve as it drives forward. When we negotiate a curve we describe the arc of that turn by orienting our front wheels so that the tires are tangent to the arc of that turn.

Although we may no longer think of it (we probably did when we were first learning to drive and found ourselves driving over curbs), because of the geometry of the vehicle, the rear tires generally follow the front tires except that they define a smaller arc. The difference between the arc defined by the front tires and that defined by the rear tires is known as "rear wheel cheat." This rear wheel cheat can be up to 36 inches in a large sedan. This phenomenon is evident when we see a vehicle with a very long wheel base (like a semi truck and trailer) which has a sign on the rear which warns, "Caution – Wide turns."

When the vehicle is backing around the same curve we find another phenomenon. In this case the leading (rear) tire is tangent to the arc of the turn. Since the leading tire is a rear tire, and since the orientation of the rear wheel is fixed, the front tire now describes a larger arc. In effect, the front end "swings out."

CASTER

Another factor which makes backing a vehicle difficult is caster. Caster is built into the geometry of the front wheels' attachment to the vehicle. It is easily understood by examining the wheels (casters) on a grocery cart or on an office chair. Pushing in one direction you will see that the wheels orient themselves so that the point where the wheel is attached to the cart or chair is forward of the point where the wheel touches the ground. This is known as "positive caster." When you push the cart or chair in the opposite direction you will see the wheels turn around so they will again be in positive caster. Caster is also built into the front wheels of a car, truck, or van. Its effect is to stabilize steering when the vehicle is moving forward. If you let go of the steering wheel on a straight stretch of road, the vehicle continues traveling in a straight line. When you turn a corner and then let go of the steering wheel the vehicle straightens itself. This is the result of caster and is caused by the front wheels constantly trying to return to positive caster.

When backing the vehicle, the front wheels are also trying to return to positive caster. This means that, if they could, they would turn 180 degrees just like the wheels on the grocery cart or the office chair. Because of the manner in which they are attached to the vehicle, they cannot turn completely around but, if you let go of the steering wheel, they will turn as far as their mechanical attachment will allow.   This feature, which is a stabilizing influence as the vehicle moves forward, is a destabilizing factor as the vehicle is backed. Therefore, it is critical that you not let go of the steering wheel when backing at speed.

WEIGHT TRANSFER

Another factor is weight transfer.   As mentioned earlier, when a vehicle accelerates going forward the center of gravity shifts to the rear. This increases the size of the rear tire contact patches and decreases the size of the front tire contact patches.   In REVERSE, the opposite happens. The weight shifts to the front of the vehicle.   The front tire contact patches increase in size, putting more rubber in contact with the road. The traction in front is increased. Any input to the steering wheel will have a magnified effect on the steering of the car. This also means that you are less likely to induce an acceleration skid when backing a front wheel driven vehicle.

When slowing in REVERSE, the weight shifts to the rear tires. The brake bias valve proportions the greater stopping power to the front wheels since these are the wheels which require the greatest amount of stopping power when driving forward. When slowing or stopping in REVERSE front tire traction is reduced yet the majority of brake pressure is still being applied to the front. It is very easy to induce a front tire braking skid. If any steering at all is added, the vehicle will tend to spin around the rear tires resulting in a loss of control. Therefore, it is critical to be sensitive to the tendency for front wheel lock-up when slowing in REVERSE.

All of this means that it is more difficult to drive a car in REVERSE than in a forward gear. The final and most significant reason that we cannot control a car in REVERSE as well as we can in a forward gear is because we rarely practice it. We found that with minimal practice, students are able to show vast improvement in their ability to back a car quickly and under control.

Generally, if you are required to back out of a threatening situation you will be under considerable mental pressure. You can assume that you will experience tunnel vision and the loss of fine and complex motor skills. Backing at speed is difficult enough without compounding the problem with these additional considerations. Your response must take these factors into account. If the obvious problem is to your front (and we assume that is why you want to back the car), tunnel vision may cause you to stare directly at the problem to the front. This may, in fact, be the distraction. You must, therefore, force yourself to break tunnel vision and look for threats from the sides and rear. If the trap has been slammed shut by an assailant driving right up to your rear bumper, backing may no longer be a viable option. (Of course you should have already been aware of that vehicle closing in on you.)

If you are going to back up, first put the car in REVERSE.

We saw the next step forgotten so often in the excitement of a simulated attack that we made it an often repeated rule. "If you are going to back up, first put the car in REVERSE." Unfortunately, placing the car in REVERSE requires both fine and complex motor skills. Students who have been driving for decades are often surprised by their inability to shift from DRIVE to REVERSE under stress. Under normal circumstances most drivers routinely shift into

REVERSE without giving it a thought. If they were to think about it, they would realize that, in an automatic transmission vehicle with a column mounted shifter, they will pull the gear selector toward the rear of the car, and move it up two notches, and then let the lever go forward. The first notch is NEUTRAL and the second is REVERSE.

Moving the selector two notches and then stopping is difficult when stress is added to the equation. It requires those fine and complex motor skills that have now abandoned us. They have been replaced by increased gross motor skills. We have seen excited students bend the gear shift lever as they repeatedly jammed the transmission first into PARK, then down to LOW DRIVE, and back to PARK. They were unable to stop anywhere between the two extreme positions.

In order to counter the problems inherent in the loss of fine and complex motor skills you should shift in a way that minimizes the need for these skills and takes advantage of the fact that your gross motor skills are enhanced.

In a car with a column mounted gear selector, with the selector in DRIVE and the brake depressed, with your palm facing toward the front of the car, push the selector forward and up. It will go to the NEUTRAL position and stop. Now reverse your hand so that your palm faces you, and pull the selector toward your body and move it up one notch. The car is now in REVERSE. Do not pull the selector all the way into PARK.

In a vehicle with a floor mounted shifter the driver usually presses the button on the selector and pushes the lever forward two notches – past NEUTRAL into REVERSE.

In a vehicle with a floor mounted gear selector, with the selector in DRIVE and brake depressed, without depressing the button on the gear selector, push the selector forward. It will move to the NEUTRAL position and stop. Now press the button and push the selector forward one notch. The car is now in REVERSE.

NOTE: Most, but not all automatics operate as described. Check the vehicle you will be driving to ensure that this technique is applicable.

These techniques are significantly easier when you are under stress but must be practiced routinely.

Similar results could be obtained by moving the selector all the way up (column mounted shift) or forward (floor mounted shift) into PARK and then down (column) or back (floor) one notch to REVERSE. We do not recommend this technique, however. In an emergency requiring moving we never want the transmission in PARK. Although we routinely take the car out of PARK without conscious thought in our routine driving, when surprised many people forget to depress the brake. You will be unable to move the selector from PARK unless the brake is depressed.

If your car stalls when backing you must place the transmission in either NEUTRAL or PARK to restart the engine. If the car is rolling, it is better to start the car in NEUTRAL. You would have to stop the vehicle completely before you could shift into PARK. Restarting in NEUTRAL will allow you to continue rolling away from the threat.

When you shift from REVERSE to DRIVE, push the selector down (forward on a floor mounted shift) with your palm forward. The selector will go through NEUTRAL and stop in DRIVE.

If you can back in a straight line, you can choose from at least three techniques. If you must back around a curve you will be limited to the over the shoulder technique below.

LOOKING FORWARD TECHNIQUE

Having stopped, looked to the sides and rear, and shifted into REVERSE, pick a spot directly to your front. I find it preferable to pick a spot well to the front because it makes it more likely that the point selected is directly to the front. Others advocate looking at a closer point since this is where the threat is more likely to be. Whichever you find preferable, focus on the spot you choose. With your hands on the steering wheel at the normal 9:00 and 3:00 o'clock position, accelerate. If you drove straight to the point where you stopped, and if you are backing straight to the rear, you should only have to hold the steering wheel steady. There will be no need for radical inputs. Most people find this technique unnatural but not difficult. With a little practice you will soon be able to back as fast as the vehicle will allow. Back until you can safely turn around and evade.

This is often the best technique to use in the dark. Backup lights do not provide near the light that the headlights do, making it much easier to see to the front. If the threat is to the front, using this technique will allow you to keep it in sight.

REARVIEW MIRROR TECHNIQUE

Having stopped, checked the situation to the sides and rear, and shifted into REVERSE, pick a spot directly to your rear (in the rearview mirror). Be sure to pick a spot well to the rear. If you choose a relatively close aiming point you will find that it disappears from view as soon as you accelerate because of the weight shift. Because accelerating in REVERSE causes the front of the vehicle to dip and the rear to rise, a point close to the rear will be blocked by the rear of the vehicle.   Picking a point too close to the vehicle also means that you will quickly run over the point and will have to select another. It is also preferable to pick a spot well to the rear because it makes it more likely that the point selected is directly behind you. Focus on this spot in the rearview mirror. If you glance away you may find it difficult to reacquire your aiming point. With your hands on the steering wheel at the normal 9:00 and 3:00 o'clock positions, accelerate.   If you drove straight to the point where you stopped, and if you are backing straight to the rear, you should only have to hold the steering wheel steady. There will be no need for radical inputs.   Most people find this technique counterintuitive but not difficult.   With a little practice you will soon be able to back as fast as the vehicle will allow. Back until you can safely turn around and evade.

This technique may be the best to use if the windshield has been hit and the spider webbing has reduced vision to the front.   It may also be the preferred technique if there are obstacles to the rear that must be avoided.

OVER THE SHOULDER TECHNIQUE

Having stopped, looked to the sides and rear, and shifted into REVERSE, place your left hand at 12:00 o'clock on the steering wheel.   This will allow maximum movement to the right and left. This is the one exception to the no palming the wheel rule. Palming may be required in hard turns to keep your hand at 12:00 o'clock. Do not release the wheel. If you do, the effect of caster will be to turn the vehicle rapidly. Turn your torso to your right (in a left hand driven vehicle). Grasp the passenger seat to anchor yourself. Push yourself up off the seat by pressing on the dead pedal with your left foot and straightening your left leg. Looking through the back window, drive to the rear. If you drove straight into the point where you stopped, and if you are backing straight to the rear, you should only have to hold the steering wheel steady. Most people find this technique the most natural but are not used to backing at speed. With a little practice you will soon be able to back in a straight line as fast as the vehicle will allow. This is the only one of the three techniques that can be used to back around a curve. If you must apply inputs to the wheel, make sure that they are smooth. Remember, because of front end swing out, remain as close to the inside of the curve as possible. Even though many find this the most natural of the techniques, most also find it the most difficult because their body is contorted and they are steering with only one hand. This technique will require more practice than the others. Back until you can safely turn the car around and evade.

As stated above, this is the only one of these techniques that can be used to back around a curve. A disadvantage of this technique is that you will have to rise up out of the seat in order to see adequately. This may make you an easier target.

Many newer cars have governors or "rev limiters" which limit the vehicle's speed in REVERSE. In some vehicles the maximum speed is reduced to as little as 18 to 20 miles per hour. You must determine how fast your vehicle will go before the emergency. You will not want to try to escape at a speed so slow that the assailant can keep up with you on foot.

SIDE MIRROR TECHNIQUE

A final option is to use the side mirrors. Most people find this to be the most difficult. It should probably be used only if it is impossible to use one of the other techniques because of physical limitations, obstructions, or other factors. On a curve, this requires the driver to shift his view so that he is always using the mirror to the inside of the turn. This may mean constantly shifting focus as the road turns first one way, then the other. This is difficult to accomplish at speed.

AVOID BACKING

Having established that driving a vehicle backwards is more difficult that driving it forward, it makes sense to try to avoid backing at times when an attack is possible. As mentioned in the chapter on DRIVING HABITS, when you are about to park you have the advantage of being inside an operating vehicle, ready to avoid, evade, or counter a threat. You have the relative luxury of being able to survey your surroundings before getting out of the vehicle. If you have to either back in or back out of a parking space, it makes sense to do the backing when you enjoy the advantages of knowing you have checked out the area. Therefore, whenever it is practical you should back into the parking space to allow you to drive forward as you leave the space later.

EPILOGUE

The purpose of this book is to make you safer and keep you alive. Now that you have finished the book, refer back to it frequently.

As mentioned in the introduction, the *principles and philosophy* behind this approach to personal security are very different from most traditional methods. While many have taught and written about various techniques to counter threats, I have long felt that the fundamental question for the individual faced with a criminal or terrorist threat should not be what to do after an attack is initiated but how to foresee danger and avoid or evade it. The easiest way to solve most problems is to anticipate and avoid them. If one casualty can be prevented by the concepts offered here, my efforts will have been successful.

Understanding the tactics of terrorists and other criminals is an essential step in developing your own means of avoiding or evading their threats. Those tactics include the universal use of some form of *the attack cycle*. Having an appropriate doctrine to oppose those tactics is also critical. To be effective your response must take into account the immutable laws of physiology and psychology. This requires an understanding of the science behind *the color codes* and requires the development of *habits,* especially as applied to *observation skills.* Because of the high probability of an attack against targets in transit, emphasis should be placed on *driving basics, driving habits,* and *vehicle dynamics.* Finally, *high* *performance (*evasive*) driving* and vehicle *backing* skills may be required to evade an unavoidable threat.

Commentary driving, and the technique discussed for *awareness and analysis* are among the best available methods for uncovering an imminent attack. Area familiarization, *route analysis* and *surveillance detection* are among the best methods for exposing an attack planned against a specific individual. Practice these techniques until they become second nature.

This book has only touched on the subject of personal security. Others have provided lists of precautions to take in specific environments (at home, in the office, in the car, at the airport, in the airplane, at the hotel, etc.) and tactics to employ in specific types of attacks (home invasion, domestic violence, sexual assault, robbery, kidnapping, active shooter, etc.). This book has covered the more important personal security issue - how to spot danger *before* it becomes a life-threatening matter. As long as people are being victimized there is a need for tactics and techniques to avoid and evade terrorists and other violent criminals.

Please email any comments, suggestions, corrections, or questions to me at richardnbradford@gmail.com. I look forward to hearing from you.

Prepare for the unexpected.

GLOSSARY

Apex – That point in a turn where the inside tires come as close as possible to the inside edge of the available road surface. Also know as the "clipping point."

Attack cycle - A sequence of events used to plan and execute an attack against personnel or facilities.

Caster – The mechanical design that causes the front wheels of a vehicle to straighten. Caster is a stabilizing influence on a car being driven forward. It is a destabilizing influence when in reverse.

Clipping point - See "Apex."

Color code - A system used to categorize various levels of awareness.

Commentary driving - A technique that aids awareness by describing your environment aloud as you drive.

Complex motor skills - The skills necessary to accomplish coordinated muscle and nerve activities in order to accomplish a task.

Confirmation bias - The tendency to perceive things as we want or expect them to be.

Cover - Protection from small arms fire.

Cover (for action) – An obvious ostensible (but false) reason for your being somewhere or doing something. For example, the cover for standing at a bus stop is waiting for a bus. The actual reason for being there may be to conduct surveillance or to execute an attack.

Decreasing radius turn – A corner in which more steering is required as the corner is negotiated. This may be a result of either the configuration of the road itself or of a driving line which requires more steering as the exit is approached. These turns are generally "fast in – slow out."

Entry – That point where the outside tires turn in from the outside edge of the available road space as a vehicle begins turning into a corner. Also known as "turn in" or "turn in point."

ESCAPE(D) - A mnemonic used in observing and analyzing an environment for personal security issues. The letters represent environment, scan, cover and concealment, allies, potential threats, entrances and exits, and distance.

Exit – That point where the outside tires return to the outer edge of the available road space as a vehicle completes a turn. Also know as "track out."

Fine motor skills - The dexterity necessary to coordinate and execute movement of small muscles such as those in the fingers and wrists.

Foveal vision - The approximately one degree of vision in the center of the retina where color and detail are clear.

Front end swing out – The condition caused by the fact that the front tires will describe a larger arc than do the rear tires in a reversing turn.

Geometric line – A driving line in which the turn begins at the outer edge of the available road space (entry) and, using a constant amount of turn, clips the inside edge (geometric apex), and the outside edge (exit), without changing the initial turn of the wheel. It is used to maintain the speed developed in the long straight leading into the corner.

Gross motor skills - The skills necessary for the movement of large muscles such as those in the torso, arms, and legs.

Hard target - A well protected relatively invulnerable target.

Increasing radius turn – A corner in which less steering is required as the corner is negotiated. This may be a result of either the configuration of the road itself or of a driving line which allows less steering as the exit is approached. These turns are generally "slow in – fast out."

Late apex, increasing radius, or ideal line – A driving line in which the entry, apex, and exit are all later than would be the case in a geometric turn. It is used to allow earlier acceleration onto a long straight following the corner.

Limit of adhesion – As fast as a vehicle will accelerate, brake, and/or corner (either singly or in combination) without inducing a skid.

Limit point – The farthest point to which you have an unobstructed view of the road.

Neural pathway - A part of a complex of nerve cells which connects the brain with other parts of the body. A habit.

Over steer skid – A condition in which the rear tires have lost traction. The result is a tendency for the rear of the car to slide in the direction of the steering input. The car is over reacting to the steering input. Also known as "fish tailing." (See under steer skid.)

Peripheral vision - The approximately 170 degrees of monochromatic unclear vision in the periphery of the retina.

Rear wheel cheat – The condition caused by the fact that the rear tires will describe a smaller arc than do the front tires in a forward turn.

Safe haven – A place where the potential victim of an attack may go but where attackers would probably not go.

Shuffle steering – Steering by passing the wheel from hand to hand. When shuffle steering your right hand always remains on the right half of the steering wheel and your left hand always stays on the left half.

Soft target - A relatively unprotected and vulnerable target.

Street line – That driving line which makes maximum use of the available road space (your lane) and complies with all traffic regulations.

Tactical parking – Backing into a parking space to allow driving forward when leaving.

Target of opportunity - The target of an attack usually selected because of a vulnerability, often a lack of awareness or visible protection.

Threshold braking – A technique in which the amount of the pressure applied to the brake maximizes stopping ability. The threshold is that point just short of locking the wheels (losing traction). The importance of threshold braking has decreased with the advent of the anti-lock braking system (ABS)

Track out - See "Exit."

Trail braking – A technique in which some pressure is applied to the brake pedal as the car is turned. The purpose is to increase the weight on the front tires. This increases the available traction in the front, or steering tires. It is employed to avoid an under steer skid.

Tunnel vision - The tendency to focus on a single object or activity. Tunnel vision maximizes the use of foveal vision and minimizes peripheral vision.

Under steer skid – A condition in which the front tires have lost traction. The result is a tendency for the car to continue going straight in spite of steering input. The car is under reacting to the steering input. Also known as "pushing" and "plowing." (See over steer skid.)

BIBLIOGRAPHY

Bernard Design Inc. (2001), *The Interactive Guide to High Performance Driving: Novice Edition.* [DVD]. http://www.hpdguide.com.

Coyne, Philip; Penny Mares, and Barbara MacDonald, *Roadcraft: the Police Drive's Handbook.* London, The Stationary Office, 2007.

de Becker, Gavin, Tom Taylor, Jeff Marquart, *Just 2 Seconds: Using Time and Space to Defeat Assassins.* Studio City, CA, The Gavin deBecker Center for the Study and Reduction of Violence, 2008.

de Becker, Gavin, *The Gift of Fear: Survival Signals That Protect Us From Violence.* New York, NY, Random House, Inc. 1997.

Duhigg, Charles, *The Power of Habit: Why We Do What We Do in Life and Business.* New York, NY, Random HouseTrade Paperback Edition, 2014.

Gigerenzer, Gerd, *Gut Feelings: The Intelligence of the Unconscious.* Viking Penguin, 2007.

Givens, David, *Crime Signals: How to Spot a Criminal Before You Become a Victim.* New York, NY, St. Martin's Press, 2008.

Gladwell, Malcolm, *Blink: The Power of Thinking Without Thinking.* New York, NY, Little, Brown and Company, 2005.

Grossman, David A., *On Killing: The Psychological Cost of Learning to Kill in War and Society.* New York, NY, Little, Brown and Company1996.

Johnson, Tamra, *AAA NewsRoom,* http://newsroom.aaa.com/2016/09/americans-spend-average-17600-minutes-driving-year/

Klein, Gary, *Sources of Power: How People Make Decisions*, Cambridge, MA, The MIT Press, 1998.

Klein, Gary, Ph. D., *The Power of Intuition: How to Use Your Gut Feelings to Make Better Decisions at Work*, New York, NY, Currency Books, 2003.

Lovette, Ed & Dave Spaulding, *Defensive Living: Attitudes, Tactics & Proper Handgun Use to Secure Your Personal Well-Being.* Flushing, NY, Looseleaf Law Publications, Inc., 2000.

Mills, Kenneth C., Ph. D., *Disciplined Attention: How to Improve Your Visual Attention When You Drive.* Chapel Hill, NC, Profile Press, 2005.

Navarro, Joe, *What Every Body is Saying: An ex-FBI Agent's Guide to Speed-Reading People.* New York, NY, Collins Publishers, 2008.

Ripley, Amanda, *Time Magazine*, "Alive: From hurricanes to 9/11:   What the science of evacuation reveals about how humans behave in the worst of times." May 2, 2005

Ripley, Amanda, *The Unthinkable: Who Survives When Disaster Strikes - and Why,* New York, NY, Crown Publishers, 2008.

Scottie, Anthony J., *Driving Techniques For the Professional & Non-Professional.*   Palm Coast, FL, PhotoGraphics Publishing, 2004.

Sherwood, Ben, *The Survivors Club: The Secrets and Science that Could Save Your Life*, New York, NY, Grand Central Publishing, Hachette Book Publishing, 2009.

Simons, E. J. (2003), *Surprising Studies in Visual Awareness: Volumes 1 &2.* [DVD]. Champaign, IL, Viscog Productions, http://www.viscog.com.

Van Horne, Patrick and Jason A. Riley, *Left of Bang: How the Marine Corps Combat Hunter Program Can Save Your Life*, New York, NY, Black Irish Entertainment, LLC, 2014.

Vendantam, Shankar, *The Washington Post*, "Dispatch from the Department of Human Behavior:

In Crisis, People Tend to Live, or Die, Together, September 11, 2006.

Wiseman, John "Lofty," *The SAS Survival Driver's Handbook: How to stay safe and be confident on and off the road*. London, Harper Collins Publishers, 1997.

ACKNOWLEDGEMENTS

Often in classes when I am describing confirmation bias (seeing what we want or expect to see rather than what is actually there), I refer to my wife's editing things that I have written. I believe that my thoughts and the way that I express them are pure genius. She sees gibberish. I thank her for doing her best to minimize the gibberish. Where that effort has failed it is my fault, not hers. Thank you for trying, **Elizabeth**. I greatly appreciate it even if I am forced to admit - usually you're right - I'm wrong.

A special thanks to my **fellow instructors** who participated in our many brain storming sessions. They always had great ideas to improve personal security training. Whatever success the graduates of our courses may have had they owe to this cadre.

Frank Meade provided an immense contribution to the contents of this work. His expertise and experience were particularly helpful. The advice of **Zach Grove**, President of Armada Global, Inc. and my lifelong friend **Mike Farrell** is especially appreciated. It was not possible to include all of Frank, Mike, and Zach's advice here. Hopefully, if there is sufficient interest from the readers of this book, follow-on editions or books will include more of their excellent recommendations.

A special thanks to several colleagues and friends I admire very much. They include **Red, Gunner, Ken, Rick, Jerry, Ed,** and many others.

Finally, thank you to **my students**, many of whom serve bravely and anonymously in the world's most dangerous places. Your service is no less patriotic for being unheralded.